SCHOOLS OF SHERINGHAM

the development of education in
Upper Sheringham, Lower Sheringham
and Beeston
1815 – 2004

the pathway from religious study and rigorous
rote learning to learning for life through dialogue
and encouragement

Michael D. Slipper,

M.A B.A. (Hons.), A.C.I.E. (Cambs.), A.C.P., Dip.Ed.,
Hon. Fellow School of Ed. (UEA).

*'1815 We built our school room and Charlotte established a school of 40
poor girls on the Lancastrian System principally and praised be Almighty
God it succeeded far beyond our expectation. Harry and Mary* (his son
and daughter) *are members of it. I never met with children more fond of
reading than they are.'*

From Abbot Upcher's Diary

GW00689648

Larks Press

Published by the Larks Press in association with the author.

Ordnance Farmhouse, Guist Bottom, Dereham NR20 5PF
01328 829207
larks.press@xlnmail.com
Printed at the Short Run Press, Exeter, 2015

ACKNOWLEDGEMENTS

This account of the development of educational opportunities 1815 to 2004 would be a most arid read without the refreshment provided by the memories that are scattered through the text. To those who have helped to make this potential desert into a lively oasis I offer my sincere thanks. These are listed below:

Patrick Dye – Sheringham High School (A Promise of Change)
Sheringham Community Primary School for the loan of Log Books
Sheringham Museum Trust also for Log Books
Norfolk Archive Centre for their help in directing me to the
Upchers' massive contribution
Norman Cooker for his contribution both written and advisory
Ron Pegg for the loan of Attendance Certificates
Margaret Jeffries for information on private schools

A Collection of Memories and Thoughts by a Pupil of the
Upper Sheringham School by Ron Spendloff 1993.

I am indebted to the late Ian Mercer for notes from Upper Sheringham School Logs 1904 to 1939 and 1939 to 1949 copied verbatim.
Finally my personal thanks must go to Thomas Weston, my eldest grandson, who has managed to read my scribble and create a legible script.
To all those involved I owe a great debt of gratitude.

British Library Cataloguing-in-Publication Data
A catalogue record for this book is available
from the British Library

ISBN 9781904006 78 7

FOREWORD

⇥⋅⊪⋅⇤

Mike Slipper is eminently fitted for adding a book to the Sheringham 'bookshelf', having served as Headmaster of Sheringham Primary School, and, in a wider brief, as an Ofsted inspector. He also grew up in the town and went to school here. Not only did Mike throw himself whole-heartedly into every aspect of the job, adding his own love of sport to a wide knowledge of Norfolk and its people, although he crossed a couple of county boundaries in the course of his career! This volume will be greatly enjoyed by Shannocks and by those whose birth half-qualifies them for the prestigious title.

We wish his publication well.

Alan Childs
March 2015

PREFACE

When I was asked to compile this 'story' of the education development in Upper Sheringham, Lower Sheringham and Beeston I was flattered but pleased to accept the challenge. Later I began to wonder what the size of that challenge would be! However, in the course of my research I discovered that not only had my father attended the Upper and Lower Sheringham Schools, but many of my father's aunts and uncles. Some of these also taught at the schools.

My brother and I also attended the Infants' and Boys' Schools. We both became teachers, and in 1951 I started my career in education. My brother started some three years earlier. Roy was a secondary teacher of English with Music as a 'bolt-on' extra, while I trained for secondary work but taught primary.

I served education for 49 years at various levels and in a variety of posts from class-teacher, through three headships, an eleven-year period as County Inspector/Adviser and finally five as an OFSTED Registered Inspector.

My third headship was at Sheringham County Primary School on Cremer Street. I followed Mr A.W. James who, as Youth Leader, had suggested that I take up teaching as a career

These are my credentials, or reasons for accepting the challenge. I hope what follows will be of interest.

Before the Education Act of 1870 which made school attendance compulsory, education took place in many different ways and in many places. For example there were the orators with students sitting at their feet, the 'master' with his apprentice, learning the skills of the trade, and the scholars in ecclesiastical establishments. Some forms of more formalised education took place in earlier centuries. The text which follows will attempt to trace the educational opportunities which existed in Upper Sheringham, Lower Sheringham and Beeston from the earliest records. Present day opportunities will also be outlined and exemplified.

Michael D. Slipper M.A B.A. (Hons.), A.C.I.E. (Cambs.), A.C.P., Dip.Ed., Hon. Fellow School of Ed. (UEA).

CONTENTS

ILLUSTRATIONS

The old workhouse at Upper Sheringham, adapted as a schoolroom
by the Upcher family after 1834, now private dwellings.

The old school at Beeston,
later used by the 1st Beeston Regis Scout Troop.

AN OVERVIEW TO SET THE SCENE

General background through the 16th to 18th centuries
to the coming of the Education Act of 1870

During the 16th century, when local gentry and farmers became more prosperous, the demand for education increased. Local benefactors created endowed grammar schools which offered education to town boys while taking boarders from further afield. Two such which are well known to Sheringham were Gresham's at Holt and the Paston Grammar School at North Walsham. These were founded in 1555 and 1606 respectively. Some of these schools flourished sufficiently to become public schools, as did Gresham's at Holt.

The 18th and 19th centuries saw the provision of education develop from a very limited number of schools to a well organised national system. By the 20th century compulsory education was a well-established fact and illiteracy was disappearing.

Following the French Revolution, the English upper class saw the need for control of 'the masses'. A system was required which would teach pupils their Christian duties as well as to read and write. Further it was realised that with an extension of the franchise in 1832 the nation needed to be more literate. Workers who were better educated would be needed to operate the new industrial machines. In spite of this the belief was that education should produce God-fearing, obedient and law-abiding citizens.

In villages 'dame schools' were created, which offered an opportunity for the eighteenth century village child to have some schooling. These schools consisted of a dozen or so children in a room in a house with the 'teacher' running at times no more than a baby-sitting service. There was no system of inspection or quality control of premises or teachers. The Parliamentary Select Committee of 1834 lists a large number of such schools in Norfolk. Frequently these were short-lived establishments whose very modest charges put them beyond the reach of many.

During the eighteenth century charitable people left private endowments to set up schools for the poor. By 1816 there were 100 such schools in Norfolk. An example of the curriculum in these schools is as follows: 'teaching girls to read, knit, sew and learn their catechism'. Often endowments would specify that the children should learn 'some useful work'. The existence of these schools was patchy and could never supply education for the masses.

In the late 18th century Sunday schools began, usually for those children who had been working all week. For example in Fakenham by 1834 there were four Sunday schools: Church of England, Wesleyan, Independent and Particular Baptists. Free tuition was usually offered and was often provided by the educated, for example The Lady of the Manor or the Vicar's wife. The main strand was Bible teaching and enabling children to read that Book. Attendance at chapel or church was part of the day's proceedings.

Nothing in the foregoing was likely to tackle the task of education on a national scale. In 1811 The National Society for promoting the Education of the Poor was set up and The British and Foreign School Society followed in 1814. The former was linked to the Church of England, the latter to the non-conformist independent churches. Religious differences led to continual rivalry.

At this point it may be of interest to note that by 1816 The Select Committee estimated that just over 26,000 children in Norfolk attended school; 8,500 on Sundays only.

By 1840, 64 new schools had been built in the County and attendance doubled. However attendance was variable, depending upon the amount of work that was available in the fields, to pick vegetables and fruit in the appropriate season. Stone-picking from the beach was also a common activity. In Lower Sheringham the help required in connection with fishing is noted frequently.

From 1833 a fund of £20,000 provided government grants for building purposes. Half the total cost had to be raised locally. This fund was increased to £30,000 in 1839. In 1870 the Forster Education Act ordered the setting-up of 'Board Schools' where there were insufficient voluntary schools. Not until 1886 were there enough places available to accommodate all those children who needed to be taught.

After 1870, all parents were compelled to see that their offspring had education. By 1880, 72 Board Schools had been created in Norfolk.

Although the part played by the State in education had increased, it still had a subsidiary role in rural Norfolk. The 72 Board Schools stood alongside 126 National and 115 Voluntary schools. The British Society also set up a few rural schools. Their schools were usually set up in the richer town areas, like Wells (1838) and Dereham (1841).There was also a shortage of trained teachers as the numbers of establishments increased. To offset this, an institute for teacher training was set up in Cathedral Close, Norwich. This became the Norwich Training College which moved to Keswick Hall on the outskirts of Norwich after World War 2. The College is now the School of Education and is part of the University of East Anglia.

The difficulty of ensuring that 'compulsory' really meant what it said will unfold as the local educational scene is described in the following pages. This challenge alongside the changing curriculum and the varying needs of society will also become apparent.

A final reminder: until relatively recently 'education' was seen as something that happened at school and for the majority finished at the age of 14. Now it is accepted that it is a life-long process.

PART ONE

EDUCATION IN SHERINGHAM AND BEESTON
1815 TO 1945

In following the development of education it is essential to place it in the context of the general picture. For example one might consider the school set up by Charlotte and Abbot Upcher to be a 'Dame School', but the following extract from *'The Recollections of Emma Piggot (née Upcher)'* may modify your view of the Upcher School.

I do not think there is much to make a story of in the next few years of life at Sheringham - the years of the school lessons.

We always began the day by learning verses from the Bible, which we repeated to our mother before breakfast. We learned a great deal of poetry, which even now furnishes one's mind with many beautiful thoughts, and which I think of great value in the education of children, as it refines and cultivates the mind. We used to hear a great deal read by our mother, who was unequalled both in natural beauty of voice and manner as a reader, and who had so highly intellectual a mind that, without teaching, she was our best teacher. Her power of conversation was unusual; she preferred speaking of things rather than people, and hated anything like gossip or censoriousness. She would never allow us to talk of what we were eating at dinner, so that when I grew up, I used to feel quite uncomfortable if I heard any conversation on such subjects.

In Winter evenings we all sat round the table working while she read, and thus we learned a great deal of history and other things. In those days we had no lamps, and two tall tallow mould candles, in high old-fashioned silver candlesticks, were all that was allowed to light our whole party, and these required snuffing about every ten minutes. But very early we had another training, in which example largely assisted. I think from the time we were ten years old we had classes in the Sunday School, and in the evenings helped our mother with the adult, or, as she called it, the Hobbledehoy-school, and many men were taught to read by us.

For nearly forty years I was seldom without a class. Then I felt I had taught myself out, and gladly passed on the mantle received by me from my mother, hoping it might drop with still more power upon my daughters, and I am thankful to believe that this is the case.
Written between 1814 and 1820.

In the beginning.....

Before compulsory schooling for all became law in 1870 the majority of people had little opportunity to become literate. There were Sunday Schools created by the churches. These were mainly for children who worked in such places as factories during the week. In Upper Sheringham it was only the children of the 'better-off' who could attend Gresham's School. In fact during the 19th century 30 children from Upper Sheringham attended Gresham's.

When the Upchers moved into their new estate in 1812 there was no school of any kind in Upper Sheringham, Lower Sheringham or Beeston. These last two were still at an early stage of their development, very much fishing villages, with some farming adjoining. However in 1814 Charlotte Upcher felt that there was a need to educate the young of the village of Upper Sheringham. She found the money to provide for the education of several girls. The following year Mr Abbot Upcher had a school room built for the purpose.

His diary states: '1815 we built our school-room and Charlotte established a school of 40 poor girls on the Lancastrian system principally and praised be Almighty God it succeeded far beyond our expectation. Harry and Mary are members of it. I never met children more fond of reading than they are'.

Charlotte Upcher adds: 'Upcher built an excellent room and fitted it with everything useful and comfortable and on the 15th I had the inexpressible satisfaction and long hoped for pleasure of opening the Sheringham School which consists of 40 girls. May the Almighty Father bestow His Blessing on it.'

As can be seen from a visit to the Church of All Saints in the village, the Upchers were devout members of the Church of England. In spite of this the school was organised on a system created by Joseph Lancaster, a young Quaker (1778). He praised 'education for all' and the teaching of religion from a non-denominational point of view. He devised the 'monitorial' system where older pupils were taught by the teacher who then taught the younger ones. This avoided the need for more teachers, who would have to be paid. (A similar system was suggested in the 1980s for in-service training for teachers. On this occasion it was known as the 'cascade system').

George III supported Lancaster and the Royal Lancastrian Society was created to promote the system.

Readers may smile wryly when they read that Lancaster promoted education by 'praise and reward'. In spite of that declaration, punishment was still available for very bad behaviour. The definition of 'bad behaviour' ranged from unwashed faces to 'wandering', the punishment for this being shackles. After many years of controversy about his scheme Lancaster emigrated to America in 1818, where his methods flourished.

This controversy bi-passed Charlotte Upcher's school. The numbers attending increased to include boys. In 1836 there were 50 girls and 30 boys. The cost to parents was one penny a week (240 pence=£1 at that time) per child. The teacher was Elizabeth Shinkfield (née Rushmer). Her husband appears in the Census of 1851 as a schoolmaster in Gresham village. Attendance ceased at the age of 12. Attendance was always a problem for boys who were often needed to help with the fishing or on the land. At the age of 12 girls often went into service and boys could be bound as apprentices to learn a trade. (See examples of indentures in Sheringham Museum archive).

Soon, with an increasing realisation of the usefulness of education, although perhaps not for its own sake, plus the enthusiasm and drive of the Upchers, a larger building was needed. After the Poor Law Amendment Act of 1834, workhouses were formed into Unions. Earlier buildings continued to be used; the Erpingham Union used Upper Sheringham until 1848 and Gimingham until 1851 when a new workhouse was built at West Beckham. The latter was well known locally and continued to be used until closure in 1948. Consequently the Upper Sheringham workhouse became available as a school building to accommodate 120 pupils. Henry Ramey Upcher followed the example of his mother Charlotte in funding the school and the education of the village children.

The school now had a new master, Thomas Almond, who, with his wife Elizabeth, arrived from London in 1853. Thomas had previously taught in Essex and Middlesex. He remained Headmaster at Upper Sheringham for more than 30 years. He is still well remembered through the 'Almond Award for character', presented annually to one girl and one boy at the High School.

Edward Savage, replaced him in 1886. He came from Kent with his wife Mary and both taught in the school. They had six children, the most notable being their son Graham, who excelled at Cambridge with a double merit in History and later became Senior Inspector in Her Majesty's Inspectorate (HMI). The Savages continued to contribute to the education of Upper Sheringham pupils for over thirty years.

When the school-leaving age rose to fourteen, children from the Lower Sheringham area schools had to walk to Upper Sheringham (a distance of up to 1½ miles). A new classroom was added in 1890. The school now had a capacity of two hundred housed in three rooms:

1) 60' x 20' x 20'
2) 24' x 17' x 15'
3) 30' x 18' x 23 ½'

The school's Log Book records the 'number on roll' of all classes (Standards I-VII) as 186 in 1894. In the same year children were admitted from Lower Sheringham Infants School when in Standards IV-VII.

The rise in pupil numbers clearly charts the development of Lower Sheringham:

Year	Number on Roll
1895	209
1897	241
1899	264
1901	278
1902	267
1904	226

The school-leaving age of fourteen created some difficulties, and was unpopular with many parents, especially those from Lower Sheringham, as the wage a teenage son could earn was essential to family survival.

Overcrowding was also an increasing problem, but, in spite of this, good results were achieved as the 20th century arrived. The Log Book records *'prizes for drawing awarded in April and May 1901'*. However, in 1902 the HMI Inspector observed *'accommodation which has now become inadequate to the growing needs of the district'*. There was also a comment on 'attendance affected by the distance from home'.

In March 1902 *'the Vicar gave out three prizes given by School Newspaper'*. In January of the same year a pupil won *'an open competition for carving taught by Miss Jeffries'*. In April 1904 *'Labour Certificate Exam - seven children passed Standard VI'*.

In March 1906 *'Papers were distributed and collected to ascertain the numbers of children going to the new schools'.* On June 11th, the beginning of the academic year of 1906-07, the Upper Sheringham school had 66 pupils on roll. This school's Log Book ends 28th May 1909. Later short entries, post 1906, suggest that Mr Savage was much happier when the school was larger. He had been Headmaster for a considerable time by then and in 1928 he was forced to retire owing to his deafness. In spite of his smaller responsibility he had clearly maintained good standards as seen in the Inspectors' Report (HMI) of March 1913:

Inspectors' Report (HMI) 06.03.1913

Excellent tone in school
Regular attendance
Industrious at their work
Writing – special praise – composition of older scholars above average
Reading distinct, fluent, intelligent
Oral articulation – girls apathetic and behind boys in all respects
History and Geography well taught
Voices well trained
Children dress well
More effort required in physical exercise
Girls need practice in 'cutting and repairing' garments from home
Infants carefully and brightly taught

What was happening meanwhile at Lower Sheringham?

After the death of Abbot Upcher, Charlotte continued to show concern for education in Lower Sheringham. She had a school built on West Cliff, with a cottage for the teacher. (The buildings now form No. 10). The site was on the boundary of farmland owned by the Upchers. By 1825 there were sixty boys at the school, mainly from fishing families.

William Sims was the first schoolmaster, then from 1834 Robert Long shared teaching duties with his wife Ann Pigott. He was a fisherman before being a teacher and continued his links with the sea. When Charlotte Upcher (1838) gifted the first private lifeboat *Augusta* to Sheringham, Robert Long was its first coxswain, and served in that capacity for twenty years.

In the mid-1850s Robert and Ann Long moved to Holt. In 1845 their son Robert married Martha Middleton who became the schoolmistress. Two other teachers assisted Martha for the school roll had risen considerably. This school was replaced in 1875 by a large building at the lower end of what is now Cliff Road opposite the entry of Co-operative (now known as Co-op) Street to Beeston Road. In that year a shed was erected to the north of the old school to house the lifeboat *Augusta*. The shed was enlarged in 1894 when *Augusta* was replaced by the *Henry Ramey Upcher* lifeboat.

The new school in 1875 had accommodation for one hundred infants from Lower Sheringham and Beeston. According to the 1881 Census results there were three teachers; Mary Lown, daughter of Leonard the carpenter; Henrietta Wilson and Matilda Stolworthy from Great Yarmouth. By the beginning of the 20th century the school had two hundred pupils with another sixty in temporary accommodation. HMI had firmly criticised the 'serious over-crowding' which existed. An additional school was created (according to the Log Book) to accommodate 68 children (girls). It was first set up in the Mission Room while an 'iron building' was erected in a field off Mill Lane now Beeston Road. This was not used until 1904. The Mission Room was used from June 1903 until June 1904. The 'iron building' was used until the end of May 1906 when the new Girls' School opened on Cremer Street.

During this period, and before the building of the three schools between Cremer Street and George Street that opened in 1906, pupils aged seven and above had to walk to the school at Upper Sheringham, up to 1½ miles. This, coupled with the need for older children to earn a wage to support the family, resulted in frequent absenteeism. Other adverse factors were the need for sturdy shoes and good clothes, poor sanitation and frequent outbreaks of contagious diseases.

Once the Sheringham school was available, pupils living in Lower Sheringham could all attend the 'new' school. This left the Upper Sheringham school with a reduced roll. It remained open until 1949. The three schools, each with its own Headteacher, continued, (albeit with changes in 1957 when a Secondary School was built on the Holt Road) until 1987. It served Sheringham for eighty years.

Headteachers 1906 (on opening of School)

Boys 7-14: Mr P. Hammond-Smith
Girls 7-14: Miss L.Carnell
Infants 3-7: Miss Annie Worraker

N.B.: *An excellent description of life at the Lower Sheringham Infants' School is to be found in the recorded memories of Sheringham by Kenneth Palmer. When he was two years old he lived in a cottage at the lower end of Woodhouse Lane (Cliff Road). His memories (edited) are to be found in Peter Cox's book 'The Divided Village' ISBN 0952481057 (2000).*

Other schools in Lower Sheringham

There were several schools from the 1890s. These were small private establishments catering mainly for teenage middle-class students.

From 1892 the daughter of Thomas Almond, former Headmaster at Upper Sheringham, had a preparatory school at Fairham, Station Road. The school had moved to Knowle Road by 1896 and to Chigwell House by 1908. Both premises were on Cromer Road.

Others were:

A ladies' boarding school at Drayton House, opened in 1900, which by 1908 had increased in size.

A girls' school at Burnham House Railway (St Peter's) Road opened in 1904.

In 1904 a boys' school opened at Bromehill, Cliff Road.

During World War One there was a boys' and girls' school at Crosby House, South Street.

A boys' school also existed at The Hazard, Cliff Road.

The old farm in Morris Street (only a cottage now remains, adjacent to the car park area) was a residential school between the two world wars.

A Sunday school (now converted to a bungalow) existed on the Middle Common opposite Church Lane in Beeston. During the 1930s this was the headquarters of the 1st Beeston Troop of Scouts. (It is shown on maps circa 1928.)

More recent examples are:

In St Peter's *Church Magazine* for September 1952, there is an advertisement for Long Crendon, a boarding school for girls, which also admitted day pupils including boys. Boys were 'Prepared for all Examinations'. There was also a nursery class 'Children admitted at 3 and a half years of age'. The Principal was Mrs E.A. Badman.

Another of interest is Miss Krieger's School: Margaret Jeffries remembers:

> *I attended Miss Krieger's school from 1945 to 1952. Her first school was at Chigwell, Cromer Road - the site for the later block of flats next to The Health Centre Road.*
> *I began my schooling there mornings only, six days a week. There were two classes and Miss Krieger taught the older ones. My memories of Chigwell – warm milk at least a third full of cream – the milk must have been out in the sun or by the fire! Rolling a cabbage from a neat pile in the garden to the chickens. They were very pleased but Miss Krieger was not very pleased with me!*

The School then moved to No. 54 Cromer Road.

> *There always seemed to be lots of children around. We never had PE or Music or Creative Activities as far as I can remember.*

Miss Krieger then moved to much smaller premises in Garden Road.

> *We had the 3 Rs and a wonderful grounding in reading and writing. My particular memories include asking to go to the toilet just before midday as there was a cuckoo clock at the top of the stairs – fascinating to watch! Listening to Charles Dickens 'Christmas Carol', which was read to us every Christmas during the last week of term after a little work.*

(Thanks to Margaret Jeffries for these fascinating notes.)

The School in Lower Sheringham

The school was situated on the corner where Cliff Road meets Beeston Road and extended to a point approximately opposite Co-op Street. Built in 1875 and enlarged in 1894, it provided for infant children from both Lower Sheringham and Beeston Regis, having capacity for 160 infants (4-7 years). Early photographs suggest that it was built from local flints, in keeping with similar buildings of the same period which still survive.

In 1888 Miss Alice Parnell was the schoolmistress and in 1893 she was succeeded by Miss Emily Kent. Other staff named at this time were Eleanor Cox and Louise Cox. The former was employed as a teacher under Article 68 and the latter as a 'monitor'. By 1894 Louise had also become a teacher under Article 68.

By 1891 there were 64 boys and 60 girls in the school (124). Average attendance was 106. By 1896 numbers had risen and the average attendance was 125.

In 1895 a scarlet fever epidemic is recorded. Each home where the fever was present had to produce a 'clearance certificate' before the child or children could be returned to school. At this time only 66 children were recorded as being present. Clearly this was a difficult year for the school as the Log Book shows:

January 1895	44 present
March	127 present
April	Diptheria
May 31	77 boys and 73 girls (150)
November	143 present

Many of the entries relate to the attendance of both pupils and staff. For example: *'one child arrived too late for mark this after-noon'; 'one new girl admitted'*. Names are rarely given.

Records state clearly that *'children are sent to Upper Sheringham when they are old enough'*. This was at the age of 7. Upper Sheringham School is usually called 'The Mixed School' presumably referring to the fact that it had its own village infants and also the 7- plus children from Lower Sheringham. It was also 'mixed' in the sense that it admitted both girls and boys up to the leaving age of 12. The School Log also notes that in 1897 M.L. Cox achieved Article 68. (This denotes a Pupil teacher.)

The school roll in 1897 is recorded as 84 boys and 99 girls (183). Clearly the school was becoming larger by the year and the demands of the parents and pupils greater. This reflects the development of Lower Sheringham as an increasingly popular seaside resort and tourist attraction.

In 1890 a new Headmistress was appointed, a Miss Annie Worraker. The entries in the Log now take on a different tone. Names appear in addition to reasons for absence or lateness. For example: *'doctor's certificate presented to account for absence'* and *'absent for scarlet fever (or whooping cough)'*.

In 1901 one of the teachers resigned. By 1902 absence of pupils and staff was reported by name together with reasons. There are many entries which state *'too late to be marked present'*. As a reminder, this was the year after the villages of Upper Sheringham, Lower Sheringham and Beeston became Sheringham Town. (A town requires a population of 1,000.)

In 1903 (March 20) a report from HMI stated that there was an inadequacy of accommodation and suggests that 'an iron building be built for Standards 1 and 2'. (This is probably the 'tin hut' referred to by Annie Thirtle in John Lown's book *Memories of Old Sheringham*).

The rapid expansion of school numbers and the apparent inadequacy of the accommodation reflected in the Report from HMI had several results. The Log Book records: *'June 1 1903 Mission Room* [possibly the Church Room, now flats] *and Feb.12 1904 Temporary new iron school building.'*

By January 1905 poor HMI Reports and removal of children to private schools were factors that contributed to the next major step: the creation of new schools. Some interesting options were suggested to parents who wished to remove pupils. 1. Stay and wait for improvement. 2. Transfer to Upper Sheringham. 3. Go private. Those who chose the Upper Sheringham option were often later re-admitted stating that *'Upper Sheringham is too far to go'*. Unsuitable accommodation, problems caused by the increase in local population and a hint of leadership difficulties resulted in an urgent need for new, larger and better equipped buildings.

On March 24 1906 the Log records: *'Papers distributed and collected to ascertain the numbers of children going to the new schools.'*

The existing Headmistress, Miss Worraker, opened a new Infants' School on 11 June 1906. The numbers on the roll at that time were 107. This school was one of the three schools on the Cremer Street, George Street, Barford Road site.

The effect of the new schools in Lower Sheringham on the Upper Sheringham School

The nature of the accommodation at the Village School, formerly a workhouse, was criticised by Inspectors in 1902 in spite of considerable attempts to make improvements. A plan of 1893 shows the school to consist of two rooms – a room of dimensions 24'x17' and a schoolroom of 60'x20'. The rest of the building was dwelling space. There was also an infants' room of 18'x30' and one lavatory adjacent to the schoolrooms. This was a 'night soil' bucket arrangement. Clearly this situation was inadequate. In August 1893 plans were approved to create separate blocks for boys' and girls' 'offices'. There were three toilets for girls and one for infants with a fence between them and the boys, who had five toilets; all were connected to a cesspit. Roofs were of a design with louvre vents in glass. At this time the need to create new accommodation became even more apparent. The school roll was now 209 pupils (1895).

The fact that the accommodation was so restricted and the age range was from infants (both from Upper Sheringham and the outlying villages) up to children aged fourteen from the villages and Lower Sheringham, emphasises the difficulties. Coupled with this the Log Book begins to record 'trouble' between the girls and boys on the road between the school in Upper Sheringham and their homes in Lower Sheringham, a walk of 1½ miles each way. Absences due to inadequate boots and clothing in bad weather and a 'shortage of stationery' are also recorded.

Perhaps a final blow appears in 1905 when an invitation to Lower Sheringham's proposed 'Cookery Centre for Girls' arrived. The Managers agreed to postpone Upper Sheringham's involvement until the new schools were built.

The Prelude to the Opening of the Schools in 'urban' Sheringham

1906 came and the Managers' Log records: 'Not more than sixty children must be expected following the opening of the new schools in urban Sheringham'

Other reductions followed. Teaching staff was reduced to three, (Mr and Mrs Savage and Miss Hill). There was also a reduction in other staff to just a caretaker at £10 10s. per annum. (The caretaker also had the job of emptying the toilets. Upper Sheringham had no water-supply until the early 1950s. Water was collected at the fountain in front of the church.)

In August 1906 the possible transfer of some pupils from Bodham School to Upper Sheringham was suggested by Norfolk County Council; Bodham Managers were not at all happy about this plan, and the transfer did not happen.

Salary discussions were raised as the school was downgraded to Grade II and it was not until October 14th, 1906 that this issue was settled. This kind of problem ran on past the opening dates of the new schools in urban Sheringham – salaries, insurance and transfers. These issues overrode all else. Nevertheless there seem to have been additional 'relationship difficulties' between the schools for some years following.

Records show that on 31st May 1905: 'The children from urban Sheringham leave this school today and will attend the new council schools'. June 11th: '66 children on books'.

In spite of Mr Savage's disappointment at the reduction of this school roll from two hundred plus down to sixty-six he records a happier fact. 'E.G Savage [his son] *gains a double first in History at Cambridge'*.

From this point onward the Log Book entries, previously very full, averaged only three per page. A trickle of children leaving for the urban Sheringham schools is recorded throughout the following years. Clearly the local educational pattern was changing and space became a necessity, especially for younger infants. The 'new' schools had this.

For 1908 HMI reports: *'It is advisable that the Infants' school should be transferred to the larger classroom in order that they should have more room for marching, games etc...'* W.Hillman, HMI.

A similar pattern emerges today when schools reorganise and are often reduced in size. These same difficulties are arising in 2000+ with the return of Norfolk First and Middle schools to Infant/Junior and Primary with transfer at 11+. Overcrowding is a factor, and this occurred with the Infants' School in Cliff Road. Older pupils went to the 'tin hut' in a field off Beeston Road (then called Mill Lane).

The Upper Sheringham School continued until 1928 under the leadership of Mr Savage. He eventually retired in that year and was succeeded by Mrs Garwood.

Further entries in the Managers' Log suggest a shortage of materials and books (May 5th, 1920).

a. Note to Miss Upcher from E.G. Savage thanking her for books, *'such timely assistance in these days and believe me, Yours Obediently'*

b. *'108 books given by Sir John Draper and a typed catalogue'*. This refers to the above.

In July 1948 *'numbers so low, parents will be consulted - re the future of the school'*.

July 28th 1949: The final decision to close the Upper Sheringham School came. The Managers' Log records: *'Although no record of the starting of the schools has been formed it must be about one hundred years since the buildings were transformed from a workhouse to a school by W.H.R Upcher'* (Henry Ramey).

It adds: 'The school has prospered under masters and mistresses who gave loyal and devoted work and many well trained and taught scholars and useful citizens have been sent out. Headmasters and Headmistresses have been:

Mr L.W. Almond

Mr E.G. Savage

Mrs Garwood

Miss Williamson

Signed: H.E. Upcher'

N.B. *During the lifetime of the school much had happened in education. The Upper Sheringham School had played its part not only locally (in 1928 a Village Library was set up) but also nationally, in 1932, with G.G.Savage (a former pupil) becoming Chief HMI (Technical Education) and in the following year E.S. Savage was appointed Senior Chief HMI.*

Anyone reading the foregoing will easily see the debt owed to the Upcher family from 1814 to 1949. (Perhaps the Upper Sheringham School should be known as Upchers' School?) However, the family's relationship with the residents of Upper and Lower Sheringham was of a remarkable kind for the age. The family really cared for the welfare of their perceived constituents, providing help both financial and personal to all who needed it.

The Modern Age – Towards the Welfare State

David Lloyd George, the Liberal politician, used highly charged images to describe the wealthy opponents who stood in the way of his proposed social reforms. He compared them with 'the old workman having to find his way to the gates of the lamb, bleeding and footsore, through the brambles and thorns of poverty'.

In almost all industrialised countries during this period, sickness and old age equalled destitution. Some were provided for by funds issued by their trade unions, a few had pensions or retirement homes given by enlightened employers, others were offered alms-houses. But most poor workers once they became unemployable had to depend upon the good will of their family, soup kitchens, the Salvation Army and offerings from charities and the Church. In Britain, Poor Laws offered assistance through the parish. This was available in Upper and Lower Sheringham. There was also the Upcher family whose concern and generosity ranged across many areas as mentioned earlier. But much of this aid was rudimentary; it included accommodation in workhouses where orphans were mixed with the aged, the sick and the mentally ill.

The ethos at the end of the century was that if you were poor and unemployed you were either feeble or 'unworthy'. Public assistance was not far short of punishment. But this attitude was changing. An increasing number of people were coming to believe that luck came into the equation and that the poor were at the mercy of the economy. In industrialised countries where there were democratic governments, social reformers, trade unions, agitators and increased political representation by social democratic and labour parties all pressed their rulers for reform. The results are tabled below:

Year	Event
1906	Royal Commission to look at the workings of the Poor Law.
1909	Royal Commission reports and recommends: Institution of state schemes against sickness. The establishment of state-funded labour exchanges (previously funded by trade unions) Municipal boroughs and parishes to treat the old, sick mentally ill and young in separate institutions.

A minority in the Commission recommended the abolition of the Poor Law in favour of Health Committees for the sick. The Poor Law nevertheless stumbled on until the 1940s.

The greatest reforms in Britain during this era were those involving the young.

Year	Event
1904	The Inter-Departmental Committee on Physical Deterioration reported on the state of the general health of the population. (This committee was commissioned largely as a result of alarming evidence witnessed by army recruitment officers during the Boer War.)

	Recommendations: 1) School medical inspections 2) State funded meals for needy children 3) The introduction of physical exercise as part of the school curriculum.
1906	Local Education Authorities were empowered to provide free meals for school children.
1909	School Medical Service established. Previously, members of the working class saw little of doctors. Families who called upon them lived in the hope that the doctor might kindly forget to send his bill. Health facilities were scant for most of the population. After 1907 school medicals ensured the monitoring of the young. Initial findings were alarming: half had bad teeth, a third were unhygienically dirty and many suffered from ring-worm, poor sight and partial deafness.

Beyond the boundaries of the County of Norfolk.

During the period 1906 to 1986 when education was concentrated on one site between Cremer Street and George Street a number of significant events occurred. Added to this was the growing quantity of legislation which had to be taken on by schools. The previous tables illustrate some of them. There were also two World Wars 1914-1918 and 1939-1945. In 1918 women over the age of 30 years were allowed to vote. Teacher unions emerged. The Norfolk Branch of the National Union of Teachers was founded in 1904.

In both World Wars women played a vital role. As men left to fight abroad, women did work previously unthinkable for them. This happened even more in the 1939-1945 conflict.

The Electoral Commission is planning to lower the voting age to 16 as part of a drive to boost turnout and interest in the political process. This is considered to be the most positive step taken in the democratic process of this country for decades. It may not be as revolutionary as giving women the vote, or lowering the voting age from 21 to 18, but what it has the potential to do is add a whole new dimension to the political scene.

It is frequently stated that 'schools are a reflection of society'. The rapid changes of the years to come - ease of transport, greater equality of opportunity – challenged the skills of educationists.

The Schools in 'Urban' Sheringham

The 'new' schools complex between Cromer Street, George Street, New Road and Barford Road opened in 1906. The site was previously used as a recreation area. While each of the three schools had its own Headteacher and was run in accord with existing regulations, HMI always referred to them in reports as 'departments - Infant, Boys' and Girls'.

As many will recall, this was an 'island' site with little in the way of green space. There were small 'garden plots' between the Boys' and Girls' schools and the iron railings bordering George Street. The two schools mentioned were separate from the Infants' School. Entry to the Boys' School was from George Street and to the Girls' and Infants' from Cremer Street.

The girls and infants shared a large playground area; the boys' playground was quite separate and screened by a wall and a gate from the girl's playground. (The latter is well remembered!) The boys' 'building' had a separate workshop/classroom for woodwork and metal work, while the girls had a cookery room, later used as the first public library in Sheringham. It also housed the swimming pool and changing areas. All toilets were outside, the girls' backing onto the houses in New Road and the boys' onto Barford Road. These 'facilities', or 'offices' as they were called, in the old Upper Sheringham School, remained much the same during the life of these schools (1906-1987). The other buildings were three 'shelters', one for each playground used for wet playtimes. All were sent out for 'fresh air'.

As the school grew in numbers, these shelters were converted to other uses. The infants' shelter became a classroom, the girls' shelter became a staff-room and then a classroom, and the boys' shelter the school boiler house when open coal fires were replaced by central heating. (In 1976, there was still a stock of coke remaining from the time before the boilers were changed to oil-fired.)

In addition the infants had a small playground at the rear of their building bounded by a large wall on Barford Road. Further along Barford Road, towards Beeston Road, backing onto the railway line the Boys' School had allotments for rural studies. Later this was also the site of the school canteen where pupils' meals were cooked and served. The canteen finally became a storage depot for the Little Theatre costumes and props.

These facilities provided education for the pupils of Sheringham Town and the surrounding areas including Beeston for eighty years.

Date	Event
1906	Infants' School (3 plus – 7)
1906	Girls' School (7 plus –14 then 15)
1906	Boys' School (7 plus –14 then 15)
1953-86	Combined Girls' and Boys' School (7 – 15)
1986	New Primary School (4 plus –11)

These dates reflect the changes that took place in educational policies during the eighty years. Details of the emergence of the High School, the New Primary School (1986), the development of the High School VI form, the Woodfields School, the Nursery and Further Education opportunities will follow.

Eighty years in the life of three schools, then two schools and finally one Primary, cannot easily be described briefly. What follows is the author's interpretation of the contents of five Log Books and three Managers' Minute Books. While landmarks are recorded, the schools can better be remembered through the memories of former pupils. Where these are available they are included at appropriate points in the story.

Each school will be presented separately, Infants', Girls' and Boys' until that point in their history when they become a true Primary School with pupils under one Headteacher, Mr A.W. James.

Sheringham Infants' School

Any 'new' school, whether 'new' by replacement of a previous establishment or completely 'new', presents its own challenges for the Headteacher. This was indeed the case for each of the three 'new' schools. As will emerge, the challenges were less formidable for the Infant Headmistress, Miss Annie Worraker, than for her two colleagues Miss E. Miller and Mr Hammond-Smith.

Moving into a new building with accommodation for 240 pupils provided great relief for Miss Worraker. She knew her staff and most of the pupils and had forged good relationships with them. She had a working curriculum seen and approved by HMI. Most importantly she had more space in which to operate. She had been in post since 1900, six years in which to establish the school in the community.

The period of her headship up to the opening of the new Infants' School on 11 June 1906 was challenged by a marked increase in numbers. This produced a lack of space, accommodation which was inadequate, staff absences and associated difficulties. In 1903 HMI highlighted these in their report. In the new surroundings Miss Worraker and the school had a fresh start and they flourished.

The next five years was a period of consolidation. As with any infant school in the early 20th century a variety of minor epidemics broke out, ailments which today are considered normal and dealt with as a matter of growing up by parents and medics. At that time, with the knowledge available, medics erred on the side of caution. The school was frequently closed by order of the School Medical Officer (SMO) in order to contain the problem. Scarlet fever and diphtheria were the worst of them, almost unheard of today.

School treats, for which a day holiday was given, are recorded together with prizes. The Log records: *'received from Jarrolds for the distribution of prizes for songs and recitation'*. Normal routine was at times abandoned for maypole dancing, with parents present. Early afternoon closures are recorded: *'closed at 3pm to enable the children to go to the circus'*. The school was a happy, parent-friendly place.

Absences increased during periods of bad weather: storms with heavy rain and snow, which were clearly more severe than in winters of the present time. During one winter, temperatures were so low that records were kept in detail for several weeks. Classroom levels were as low as 40 degrees Fahrenheit (F). Present-day classroom temperatures would be at least 60 degrees F. It should be remembered that homes and schools relied on coal or wood for fuel. The 1906 schools had open fires in the classrooms and a 'tortoise stove' in the hall or corridor. Later records, made in response to a complaint, state that the caretaker responsible for all three schools, had 24 fires to light each day during the winter. It also states that 2 tons of coal were consumed each week.

Annie Worraker was replaced as Headmistress by Mrs A. E. Tansley (the wife of the well-remembered local photographer). The new Headmistress set up a programme of 'testing' each class and in 1912 she reported *'examined and reported on the work of all classes 1-4'*. It is not clear if this was the result of the frequently reported visits of HMI or at her own instigation.

Scarlet fever was again rampant in October 1912 and in fact the school was closed on 10 December of that year *'on Medical Order'*, having been closed earlier *'for disinfecting for scarlet fever'*

(26.11.1912). Children were absent for long periods, one for 8-9 weeks, one recorded as 11 weeks, where there was a large family. These health problems continued well into 1913 when the Log recorded *'all children more or less poorly'*. At this point Mrs Tansley herself was frequently absent.

Frequent visits were made by Sir Digby Pigott whose family clearly took on an Upcher-like role. In January it is recorded that *'Miss Piggot* [sic] *sent some toys for the children'*. As a matter of interest all three schools received many benefits from the local 'well to do'.

In early 1913 wet and stormy weather again caused difficulties and measles (ordinary and German) with chickenpox caused many absences among the infants. At this time there were five staff plus the Headmistress. Of the six only two were 'certificated'. This was not unusual at this time. Some were waiting to qualify through long service; others might be waiting to attend a college course. The same situation prevailed in all three schools.

Another item of note is an entry which states *'child retained in school for another year'*. This often arose when a child had been ill or entered school late and was not considered able to cope with the demands of the Big Boys' or Big Girls' schools.

This year ended on a positive note. The Headmistress continued her examination of classes and school had become a good place to be again; *'A half-holiday for good attendance'* is awarded, and, the final touch, *'Christmas tree lighted and presents given by Lady Piggot'*. Those of us of a certain age can no doubt remember the real candles on the tree. (No question of fire risk then!)

1914 began with the first mention of 'dental inspections' and 'medical examinations'. Alongside these came more scarlet fever and a new problem, ringworm. Pupils affected were required to wear linen caps. School treats (usually arranged by Sunday Schools) continued and the examination of classes had become a termly activity. The school closed early for the summer holidays owing to low attendance through sickness and inclement weather. The Log states that 18 boys and 32 girls transferred to the Boys' and Girls' Schools.

1915 starts with 9 pupils admitted. This year shows a period of change and perhaps a different attitude toward the needs of very young children. There was, however, concern for the health of the children. The Headmistress records: *'The attendance has been very low all week, the children seem in a poor state of health and the weather is very damp'. (January) 'School closed by S.M.O. for one week'*.

Listed here are the ailments and diseases occurring, bearing in mind that until the 1960s all such had to be recorded and reported. This again emphasises that what is taken for granted in medical help now was not always so.

Mumps was now added to scarlet fever, measles, chickenpox, influenza, scabies, whooping cough, ringworm, bronchitis, diphtheria and impetigo. No wonder the school was frequently closed by order of the S.M.O.

However things were changing. The 'babies' (Reception) time-table is changed to allow them to sleep until 3 pm instead of lessons. Remember that many children were starting school at 3 years of age. The times of school were changed for the 'Winter Session'; 9-11.45 instead of 12 noon and 1 pm until 3 pm.

1916 started with blizzards and all children in 'the babies' room' were excluded for measles by order of the SMO. On 3 March all three schools closed owing to measles until 17 March. On 16 February the school was closed: *'The caretaker did not light the fires'*. This was an uneventful year educationally, but a terrible one as far as the children's health was concerned. There is nothing in the Log to tell us about the War (1914-18) which was going on at the time, one can only assume that life in the town at this time, especially in the schools, was affected by it. 1917 continued in a similar manner: blizzards in January, poor attendance and an enquiry from the Education Committee asking for an explanation.

The number on the roll at this time was 155. There were 22 boys and 23 girls transferred to the Boys' and Girls' Schools in September. However the year ended on a cheerful note. The school received a Christmas tree from Mr Wyndham Cremer.

1918 started as did so many, only this time rather worse. *'Snow, 7 or 8 inches fell during the night. Only 36 children attended.'* (11.01.18). There were no telegrams or telephones. Messages could not be sent to Norwich because the wires were down. As ever, they literally weathered the storm and enjoyed some more pleasurable happenings.

In February the school returned to the summer opening times and enjoyed a half-day holiday for 'Children's Home display'. In July a Miss Ward from Furzedown visited to observe teaching methods. This is perhaps an indication that the school was 'doing different', since Furzedown was a teacher training institution. Perhaps there was something worthy of note happening in the school. The entry which records this is followed by 'breaking-up entertainment'. The thought of this in 1918 perhaps supports that view.

Following the usual note of numbers transferring to the Boys' and Girls' Schools is an interesting entry: *'School closed to enable children to get blackberries at 2.10 pm, to help with the food supply'*. This entry is dated 03.10.18 with a similar one on 11.10.18 – possibly the only references in the Log to the War which ended soon after these entries.

However the joy at the ending of hostilities is shown by the entry of 7 July the following year when: *The children left school early in order to see Locker Lamson's victory loan cars which are coming through the Town at 3.30pm'*. This was followed on 31.10.19 by *'School closed today for a week's holiday according to the King's wishes that children have an extra holiday because of the end of the Great War with Germany'*. While a distant event in some ways it was clearly one which brought much privation and pain to the local population. The lasting witness to that is to be seen on the War Memorial in The Boulevard.

Having covered in some detail the development and hardships of the Infants' School, it is time to answer the question: What was happening in the schools that were really 'new'?

The Boys' and Girls' Schools 1906-1927: challenges & solutions

All schools now faced certain changes. While the Financial Year ended as before in May, the Education Committee dictated summer holidays and the dates of the three terms. It also became a requirement that schools should provide an Annual Syllabus of Work. This was to be sent during the first 10 days in May and recorded in the Committee's Annual Syllabus of Work Book. This gave the two new schools time for assessment and planning.

The Boys' School (or Department) opened with the Headmaster Mr Hammond-Smith and 4 Staff, 2 of whom were 'certificated', Mr Hammond-Smith and another and 3 who were Article 50. Two of the three were on supply.

Mr Hammond-Smith records: *'Discipline is very loose and the character of the work chaos owing to the children coming from three schools. The intelligence is fair'*. (The three schools were: Infants, Upper Sheringham and the temporary school). He adds: *'there appears to be two distinct divisions in the school, the Upper Standards (4 to 7) being rough but intelligent and the rest in absolutely wretched condition. Standard 2 wrote a Composition on The School and of the results 50% unintelligently performed'*.

Standard 2 would be some of the youngest children who had just been admitted. (Little has changed; receiving schools frequently expect 'finished' articles when children start at Senior Level.) This appraisal still stood in September when Mr Smith again writes: *'A great number of boys in Standard 1 are very backward in Reading and Word Building and counting. There is a lack of phonics, letter combinations and blends, letter reversals. They are unable to understand number, tens and units. Many figure reversals (15/51).'* Mr Hammond-Smith was expecting much more than he was getting.

At this point the school was short-staffed and the classroom temperatures in the morning were at 48°F at 10.30 am. There were no fires and insufficient coal-scuttles had been supplied to the caretaker. The fact that this was regarded as an unreasonable lapse by the caretaker was clearly made known to him by the Headmaster. The Log records that *'The caretaker became insolent'*. This later resulted in the caretaker appearing before the School Managers. He was severely reprimanded. This is an example of the power held by Headteachers and Managers at that time. Mr Hammond-Smith was still not happy and records: *'Work still ordinary'*. Nevertheless he had now made a better assessment of the school as will be seen, but still did not really understand that the age of a pupil does not necessarily coincide with the expected ability level.

'The equipment for teaching singing is defective. There is no musical instrument (piano) in either department (Boys' and Girls')'. Following this comment from a visiting official, things changed. Pianos appeared and two groups of boys began handcrafts. Nevertheless Mr Hammond-Smith was not happy: *'The time between May 31 and July 31 will be spent in an endeavour to raise the 3Rs to a proper standard.'*

In the new term (September) HMI visited on three occasions and made 'several suggestions'. There were staff problems and caretaker problems but the Headmaster was now monitoring progress across his school and in 1908 his Schemes of Work were accepted by the Education Committee. As a change from curriculum problems there is a reminder of what was to be a main event in all three schools, Empire Day. *'May 22 1908 A Union Jack presented by Dr. Sumpter was hoisted followed by the singing of Empire songs.'*

During 1909 there were problems with staff, discipline and a change in timetable. HMI was again involved. Four visits by HMI resulted in the following suggestions: *'Standards 1 and 2 should be developed gradually from Infants by games, conversation and shorter lessons. There should be no formal tests. The Upper Standards should have more advanced and developed work especially in English subjects.'* A tough route but the School was at last on track.

In 1910 the death of Edward VII is recorded on May 13 and the schools are closed for the funeral.

The schools (Upper and Lower Sheringham) were renamed with Upper Sheringham being a Parish (Church) School and Lower Sheringham a Council School. To increase the availability of books a library box was created and moved between schools, the start of closer co-operation between the Boys' and Girls' Schools.

In 1911 a new building was constructed for Craftwork. Discipline was improving as was the work. While still being apt to complain about the quality of the pupils received from the Infants, Mr Hammond-Smith was much happier. With the help of the Norfolk Education Committee he instituted a system of 'Certificates of Honour' which were awarded for 'Regularity of Attendance'. These certificates were colourful and well-designed, a perfect incentive in those days. They were worth gaining.

In 1912, 1913 and 1914 there are three full HMI reports written up in the Log plus one for handcraft. These are all very positive and the school is at last functioning well although disturbed by the start of World War One, recorded in an entry on November 9: *'Mr Bond* [a teacher] *informed me last evening that he was joining 5 BNR.'* (5th Battalion Norfolk Regiment)

On January 19 1915: *'A zeppelin raid, damage to Mr Smith's cottage in Whitehall Yard'*, another sign that war had touched the town. For the next two years Mr Hammond-Smith had little to report. He had a purge on those who kept their class registers incorrectly, stating that he is making *'closer examination of all classes'* and that there is *'nothing eventful to report'*. There were staff shortages (most teachers were male at that time) and he writes *'Staff shortages, male members recruited for the army'*. There is no further mention of the War or the Armistice. However, the aftermath is clear. In March 1919 he records: *'Sickness of staff for the last 21 weeks. There have been only 5 weeks when all teachers present.'*

In 1920 there was still a paper shortage, which had not improved when the War ended. In this year the School Log records a number of events worthy of note. In July there is a note on transfer of pupils from the Infants' School, and in December a sign that the all-powerful School Managers were being over-ruled in control of staff by the Norfolk Education Committee. After no apparent discussion with them, a teacher was moved from the Boys' School to take charge of Field Dalling School. In town and school there was a problem with the gas supply, *'lights inadequate - work suffered'*. An end to a year of continuing challenges for Mr Hammond-Smith.

An end to the Headmaster's traumas was in sight. HMI had clearly heard and seen the lack of liaison with the Infants' School and suggested reciprocal visits to all three schools. Reading and written work were to be targeted. Mr Hammond-Smith records: *'Continued problems with the gas – too poor for written work. It has been like this for over a year.'* HMI was to check on the school through to 1923. At this date Reports to Parents and a Library were instituted.

In 1925 there were 9 teachers (including the head) on Staff. 5 were 'certificated', 3 'uncertificated' and there was 1 'student'.

By the time his period as Headmaster was over Mr Hammond-Smith had brought the school up to an acceptable standard. HMI expressed pleasure with the work, some of which was described as *'delightful'*. They also stated that *'considerable progress had been made since 1909'*.

What was happening in the Girls' School during these formative years?

Sheringham Girls' School opened in 1906 with 161 girls on roll. Miss L. Carnell was the Headmistress and had 4 staff to assist her. Miss Carnell was a 'certificated' teacher, her other members of staff were 3 'uncertificated' mistresses and a 'supplementary assistant'.

There was a regular flow of visitors to see the new buildings including HMI, 'a Minister of Education' (no name is recorded) and a County Inspector.

Difficulties arose early; there was a shortage of books. It appears that books and equipment were not available prior to the opening of the school even though the syllabus for the current year had been sent to the Education Committee. Two girls left to attend the workhouse at Beckham and one member of staff was sent to Upper Sheringham since she was unable to cope with the older girls.

Then similar challenges to those experienced by the Boys' School arose. The Headmistress complained to Miss Worraker (Headmistress of the Infants) that 3 girls did not know their letters or figures. A request to *'have them back'* was refused. Another 6 were regarded as not ready for Standard 1 work. Staff difficulties continue and HMI state that there are some staff weaknesses. A severe difference of opinion ensued between Managers and HMI. The whole stressful episode made Miss Carnell unwell. She had a series of absences when a 'certificated supply teacher', Miss Miller, ran the school.

On April 27 1908 Mary Park took over the school. She made changes in the timetable. She decided that insufficient time was being spent on practical subjects. *'Temporary changes in the timetable for Standards 5, 6 and 7 in order to give a disproportionate amount of time to needlework, which I think is advisable for a week or two.'* There is also mention of teachers' Record Books. She then began to look into standards in arithmetic and composition. Mary Park was coming to terms with the needs of her pupils and progress was made.

There is then a mention of some 'togetherness' for the three schools. On May 22 all 3 schools congregated for Empire day. They hoisted a Union Jack to which the scholars had contributed.

On June 22 an 'Opening of The Season' was shown to girls leaving *'by Labour Certificates'*. Two girls obtained certificates and 2 others enquired about them. On July 3 three girls *'left by Labour Certificates'*.

A developing curriculum, beyond reading, writing and arithmetic, is seen: cookery took place in the old Infants' School, and there was a lending library with sufficient books to allow about half the girls to borrow one book each week. Needlework as a subject was already established. Clearly the curriculum was geared to girls entering service and can be related to the increase of Sheringham's visitors, hotels and second homes for holidays. However, the Inspector recommended that 'brushwork' be added to the drawing as soon as possible.

In spite of her efforts Miss Park experienced problems similar to those of her Boys' School colleague. She was concerned by the lack of quality in much of the teaching. She led by example and gave 'criticism' lessons with all staff of the two lower standards present. The standard of teaching was such that the County Inspector recommended that the Headmistress ask the Managers to stop the teachers' annual increase in salary. As in the Boys' School the Managers were not pleased. Nevertheless HMI complimented Miss Park on her work since her appointment. They stated that discipline was now satisfactory, the industry of the girls was marked, but they warned at the same time that the Headmistress was overtaxing her strength in her efforts to maintain a uniform standard of work. After several bouts of illness Miss Mary Park retired on 24 June 1910.

Common Problems: both schools experienced severe teething problems. They were unprepared for variations in ability levels that they had not experienced before. They were not helped by the shortage of books and equipment and the lack of staff trained for what are now called 'special needs'. Experience showed them the way and they succeeded, but with some anguish and pain.

Perhaps the learning process for pupils and teachers can best be described in the words of a former pupil, Stanley Craske, who writes (late in life, but relating to the period 1920-1927):

I did not enjoy going to school until the last two years, and very few children, as far as I am aware were very keen on school. This was because our teachers were very strict and if you were a boy received the cane, either for not being able to answer a question, for untidy work or being late for school, or forgetting to call a master 'Sir'. We raced for home when the dinnertime bell went (there were no school meals in my day). Boys who had to walk in from a distance brought sandwiches wrapped in newspaper and washed the food down with water from the tap in the school yard. Sometimes we who went home asked our mums for biscuits and sweets to give to our friends who had their meals in the school playground shelters. If we saw our teachers in the Town after school hours we would go round another street to avoid them. We were all of us scared of teachers and would not dare to speak to them as modern children do.

On special days like Empire Day, they hoisted the Union Jack on a flagpole in the school yard. And we all had to salute the flag and sing patriotic songs like The National Anthem, God Bless the Prince of Wales, Land of Hope and Glory and Land of my Fathers and later on Canada and Australian songs. We always strictly observed the two minutes silence at 11 o'clock on 11 November. This was especially sad for my friends whose fathers had been killed in the trenches in France. In the last two years (1925-1927) the whole system was changed with the coming of a new Headmaster. (Mr Sidney Earcourt Day) The cane was only used on boys who bullied the younger ones. The new punishments were writing 100 lines after school or you had your cricket and football games stopped. School teams were introduced in each class named after famous people like Nelson and Wellington and good marks for your work helped your team to win a trophy at the year end.

Clearly, with the arrival of Mr Day, things changed. Lessons were learned about interest and control. A similar scenario arrived at the Girls' School with the appointment of Mrs Jessie Call in 1910. She had to take over a school which had experienced two Headmistresses in the first two years of the school's life.

By July 1910 Jessie Call had completed a review of the Girls' School in Arithmetic, Composition and Reading. She concluded that reading and arithmetic in the Upper School was 'unsatisfactory'; rules in arithmetic had not been mastered and no attempt was made *'to state sums in a practical manner.'* In composition *'ideas were good but spelling bad'*. She also criticised the apparent lack of teaching in sounds in the Lower Standards. In the light of her findings Mrs Call re-classified the entire school and reduced numbers in the Upper Standards. The previous classification seems to have been made by age rather than ability. The foregoing together with several changes of staff were factors which, according to the Log Book, *'caused the discipline and tone of the School to suffer'*. Mrs Call believed that with 'tact and management' these would soon improve.

There followed a period for her to employ tact and management. She monitored progress in all classes, the teaching as well as the learning. Records show that she gave *'special hints on teaching composition'*, following observations of lessons, and *'hints where necessary'* when examining teachers' note books (Record Books). She also invited the Drill Inspector to give demonstration lessons for staff. Note books for nature and geography were introduced. She states: *'The girls have never kept note books for these subjects before'*. The curriculum as a whole had been broadened and made more interesting. Percentage attendance figures show marked increases week on week. There was now more than the 3Rs, cookery, needlework and drawing.

This development and progress continued until 1923 when Mrs Call began to have several significant absences 'through illness'. However, the HMI report of 1924 shows that the school was thoroughly well conducted and maintained a well-earned reputation for good work. There were now regular debates arranged and conducted by the older scholars. All branches of English had improved since the previous report. It concludes with remarks about the high standard of conduct reinforced by *'the earnest work of the Headmistress and all members of her staff'*. Her work now included conferences with staff on 'Narration' (now 'Presentation') – a Headmistress with ideas about what is now called Staff Development.

During this period, in both Girls' and Boys' Schools, there are frequent references to the Almond Award. This was awarded annually to a girl and boy in each school for 'character'. The Award was in memory of Mr Almond, the first Headteacher at Upper Sheringham. The award is still made today.

It is clear from Log Book entries that Mrs Call continued to be absent at intervals, often for more than a week. This continues into 1926, until July of that year when the much loved and highly regarded teacher died suddenly. The last entry in the Log in her hand is dated 23 July 1926. Such was the affection for Jessie Call that the sum of £128 was collected for a large brass plaque to be placed in the Girls' School. This tribute can still be seen in the new Community Primary School in Cooper Road, Sheringham.

In October 1926 the School Managers appointed Miss Beatrice Hall to succeed Mrs Call. She took up her duties on 1 February 1927.

Both schools for the 7 plus girls and boys now had a new Head-teacher, each with a forward-looking attitude. We shall see the ways in which the two schools flourished and progressed during the period to the end of World War 2 later, but now, a return to life in the Infants' School.

The Infant School 1919 to 1939 – on the road to success

Perhaps it would be appropriate to look at the curriculum for infants at this time.

The 'headings' were: Nature, Reading, Writing, Colouring, Recitation and Games with a Conversational lesson, Acting of Fairy Tales, Number, Dancing/Marching/Drill. Things had clearly moved on from the days of 3Rs, drawing and the Bible. (There is no specific mention of the latter.)

There is continued evidence in the Log Books of periods of long absence and comments such as *'two children are absent whose boots are bad'*. Local dignitaries like Sir Digby and Lady Pigott are recorded as giving the children 'a tea' and similar worthy activities. Teachers from other schools visited the Infants' School for observation at the suggestion of HMI, a sure sign that they were being 'progressive' for the times. The County Inspector approved their timetables. All was going very well by April 1924 and 18 girls and 19 boys were transferred to the other schools on the site. A significant note is made that *'the Boys' Headteacher borrowed 40 Chambers Effective Introductory Readers from the Infants'* and that *'some children are kept down'*.

In 1920 there is the first mention of 'the School Nurse' visiting and examining the heads of the children. Some children were named and excluded.

Visits by teachers from other schools to observe the teaching are mentioned and *'pupil teachers absent attending interviews to attend colleges'.*

In 1921 the HMI Report states: *'This school reaches a high state of efficiency. The children are alert, happy and responsive and evidently receive a sound general training. The excellent equipment provided in the Babies Room for rest purposes deserves special mention'.*

In the next few years there is little other than routine activities. There are a number of significant historical happenings worthy of note:

26.04.23	Holiday given for Duke of York's Wedding.
26.04.24	Half-holiday for Revd Fitch's funeral (Chair of Managers and Rector of Beeston Regis)
27.11.25	Holiday for Queen Alexandra's Funeral.
29.07.26.	School closed all day for Mrs Call's Funeral (died suddenly 26.07. 26)

In 1928 the number on roll was 120. A Parents' Day was also held in that year. This is the first mention of parent involvement in any activity.

On 18 June 1928 a day's holiday was given at the 'express wish of the Prince of Wales'.

During February 1929 the school recorded a series of very low temperatures: Hall 31 degrees, Main Room 36, East classroom 40, West classroom 31. *'All fires burning brightly'.* The lowest recorded temperatures during the week 12.02.29 were 25, 26, and 27.

An indication of concern about the health of the children is given by an entry in November 1929 which states: *'Loaned to the School by Messrs Horlicks, Slough, Bucks., 1 steel cabinet, 1 gas ring, 1 urn, 1 enamel jug, 2 trays, jugs and beakers. For teachers use in making hot malted milk for the children at playtime.'*

The health situation is perhaps underlined by an entry in the Log dated 16 October 1930: *'Opening of Cromer Hospital'.* Probably this entry reflected a feeling similar to that experienced when the Norfolk and Norwich University Hospital opened some 70+ years later. Modern medicine was now available at a local Hospital.

On 30 April 1932 Mrs A.E.Tansley resigned her post as Headmistress. She had suffered periods of ill-health for some time.

On 12 September Miss Catherine Wakelin succeeded her as Head. The impact of Miss Wakelin's arrival stands out in the vibrant way the School Log is written. She introduced constructive reports on each term's work, as suggested by HMI, together with more comprehensive schemes to guide staff and put emphasis on the link between reading and language work generally – a very forward-looking set of ideas. Miss Wakelin and her colleagues, Miss Foulger and Miss Philipson (later to be Headmistress as Mrs Moores), served the school exceptionally well for many years.

Absences through illness arose again in February 1933 when, with only 43% attendance, the Schools Medical Officer closed the school for a week.

The new approach brought with it an increased emphasis on Physical Training and on January 18 1934 a visit from the County Physical Training Inspector was arranged. He spent an afternoon giving demonstration lessons from the Board of Education's new syllabus for schools for his subject. (This Syllabus was still in use in 1951 when the author began teaching.)

Sadly, on 11 January 1935 the Headmistress, Miss Wakelin, had to attend the funeral of her predecessor Mrs A.E. Tansley.

The Infants' School continued to flourish with Miss Wakelin at the helm. The recommendations of HMI had been incorporated into the school which would soon have to face up to the outbreak of World War 2 in 1939. This event is heralded by an entry of 27 September 1938 which reads: *'School closed for the purpose of assembling gas-masks in order to fit the population of Sheringham'.*

To summarise the events of this and the overlapping period to 1941 the following memories give a boy's general impression of life in both the Infants' and the Big Boys' schools:

My first memory of school is the first day that I was taken to the Infants' School by my mother at the age of four. We arrived and were seen by the Head teacher, Miss Wakelin. After what seemed forever I found myself in the first class with Miss Foulger. (I suppose this would be called Reception now). This was the only time that my mother took me to school. After that, perhaps because I made no fuss or because my mother was busy with 'visitors' a girl from the 'big' school who lived at the bottom of Priory Road took me.

School was a wonderful place to me at that time. I have fond memories of the little green beds that were brought out each afternoon for us to have a nap. I rarely slept but remember counting the roof beams and drawing with my eyes the shapes I could see. There was the lovely rocking horse on which to ride. Perhaps I remember only the good things!

Playtimes were fun, playing horses, chase and catch or taking cover in the shelters if the weather was wet.

My next teacher presented me with less happy memories. I was having difficulty with reading following a long absence through illness. One day in sheer frustration I shouted out a forbidden word and was told to wash my mouth out with carbolic soap! Not a good year! At least I could make a clean start! My next teacher was the Head teacher. I owe her much. She helped me during lunchtimes, encouraged me (with the occasional sweet) and through her giving me praise and time my reading came up to standard. I was able to transfer into 'the big boys' to be driven on by the formidable Mrs Wilton. On one occasion the choirmaster from St Peter's Church came to our class. I knew Mr Cutting through my brother Roy. I clearly remember him spotting me and saying: 'You're young Slipper. Your father is in the choir, your brother is in the choir, I shall expect to see you next Friday!' So began my involvement with choral singing and music.

Memories of the next few years are vague until I was in the 'scholarship' class with the exceptional, if volatile, Mr Cleall. He and the Head teacher Mr S. E. Day worked us hard and ensured that we had every chance of success providing that we responded to their teaching. However, just after we had taken the exam, after numerous occasions when we had to leave our classes during air raid warnings to shelter in what had been the cloakrooms, we were evacuated to various buildings in the town away from the centre. My class was placed in a house called 'Beaumont' in Hooks Hill Road. Two classes were put there. Others were at La Mouette in The Rise and Hillcrest, Abbey Road (Boys). Girls were at Corner House, Holt Road, The Vicarage, Hooks Hill and Normanhurst Hooks Hill Road. Infants were at Chancellor Cottage, Holway Road and Trevanion, The Rise. Boys and Infants from 21/04/41 and girls from 01/04/41. (M.D.S. 1933-1941)

The Boys' and Girls' Schools between the World Wars – a golden period

The Girls' School

During the period from 1927 to 1939 the Headteachers of the two schools consolidated the vital work of their predecessors. They profited from the experience gained. They were able now to deal with pupils aged 11 to 14 who had only a small desire to be at school. Many wished to be out earning a wage or helping parents with fishing and 'letting' (accommodating visitors). These years are ones of happy, productive development.

The highlights of these years were the annual Empire Day celebrations, the annual Almond Award (for character) and a growing involvement and success in local, district and (twice) national sports to name just some.

For the Girls' School it must be recorded that the late Headmistress, Mrs Jessie Call, was indeed a special person. The Log Book entry for 13.01.27 reports on her funeral at Beeston Regis that a large gathering attended including Mr S.E. Day, Mr P. Hammond-Smith, Mr and Mrs Savage (Upper Sheringham School) and Mr and Mrs Cole (East Runton School). A tribute to the *'work and devotion and ideals of Mrs Call'* was given. *'This lady was held in very high esteem'*. Further reference was made to the influence she had, *'which continues through her old pupils'*.

When Miss Beatrice Hall commenced her duties there were 145 girls in the school. Staff was Miss Hall Class 1, Miss Howes Class 2, Mrs Rollins Class 3, Miss Foulger Class 4 and Miss Campbell Class 5. (The last two named were not certificated at that time. Miss Foulger later taught in the Infants' School).

There were visits to the cinema, rambles in the woods for direct observation of nature and 'Pound Days' for Cromer Hospital (pre NHS). More significantly Miss Howes left to become Headmistress at Ashmanhaugh School (a new 'provided' school). 'The girls of Class 1 and the Headmistress carried a harp with strings of poppies to the War Memorial', the first time that such activities are mentioned (1927). The school and the community were coming together.

Other new items: 1928 Sports on the Recreation Ground (Holt Road); Open Day; 1929 Lectures in the Church Rooms (Classes 1, 2 and older girls of Class 3) in association with RSPCA; Film - Africa Today at cinema (Top classes); Netball introduced, (School

Managers provided posts, nets and ball). The girls can now use the Recreation Ground on Monday afternoon 2.30-4.30 pm.

Activities continued to expand. The use of the environment, woods, common, the beck, the shore and cliffs were now a regular feature. The presentation of a Challenge Shield by Mrs Atkinson for 'Physical Work' sharpened these activities. School assemblies were held in 'the main room' for the purpose of entertainment, each class entertaining the remainder of the school in turn.

1930 – Miss Hall did not lose sight of her main task. She found that some pupils are not coping with work in English and Arithmetic, so she reorganised the timetable so that those in that situation could work at an appropriate level. She made each member of staff responsible for a subject area. For example: Upper School (older girls) nature, drawing, singing; Lower School, nature. The Headmistress took responsibility for 'hygiene'.

A Singer sewing machine arrived from the Singer Company and a new dimension was added to the school work.

1931 – The school extended its boundaries further. A group of girls took part in the Norfolk and Norwich Festival. Twenty girls took part in a Folk Dancing Display on Saturday 16 May. This was followed later, in July, by a local display for parents and friends, *'followed by cakes made by the girls in the Cookery Centre.'* In October there was a visit to Beeston Hill for geography, *'the study of hills and valleys'.*

1932 – Continued involvement with outside activities continued. The girls joined Upper Sheringham School to travel to the Norwich Dance festival *'travelling in a charabanc'* (motor coach). One assumes that previously the train had been used.

Inter-schools netball arrived. The girls played Holt and won 14 - 4. On November 11 the Armistice Day ceremony at the Cenotaph in London was broadcast on the wireless (radio). Poppies were sold in the school.

1933 – For the new school year the Log recorded teachers' responsibilities. It is now called 'specialisation'. The year ended with *'Senior Girls' Party'.*

1934 – The School now had a roll of 173. The Schools (Boys' and Girls' combined) won the Inter-Schools Sports Shield with 57 points (Boys' contribution 15).

1933 – A syllabus for Physical Training was introduced. And in October there were exclusions for typhoid.

1935 – The Milk Scheme started. May 3, Jubilee Celebrations; June1 – The school had another success in the Inter-Schools Sports, a win with 69 points (Girls 48). Five girls took part in the County Sports at Norwich.

The emphasis on sport, dancing and other physical work brought success in sports generally and displays for parents and others became a regular occurrence. There were now 177 girls in the School. In the general curriculum there was now clear definition of responsibilities for subjects. Cookery became Domestic Science. The School was divided into 'houses' to sharpen the competitive element. Absences rose through several cases of yellow jaundice and scarlet fever.

1936 – This started with a closure for the funeral of the King (George V). In the District Sports at Cromer (for 10 schools) Sheringham was again successful. The girls gained 50½ points and the boys 25½.

A talk by the Royal Music Association resulted in musical instruments being introduced into the School.

A large group of girls, including some former pupils, visited London. The fame of the Domestic Science teaching resulted in 'The Office' sending notice that Matlaske and Alborough would visit to use 'the room' on alternate Mondays. This was also offered to Upper Sheringham, but they declined. By the end of the year there were 184 girls on roll. Several girls attended from the Children's Home. There were now termly examinations for all pupils.

1937 – The schools were now lit by gas. Miss Hall instituted annual examinations. 145 girls travelled to Cromer to view replicas of the Crown Jewels.

May 11 was a holiday for The Coronation of George VI. In September there was another excursion to London.

1938 - The funeral of the Rector of Beeston Regis, Revd Thompson took place. The combined Sports Team again won, this time with 79 points. Eye tests were introduced. In September all girls were fitted with gas-masks. On December 31 Miss Beatrice Hall retired and Miss Honora Watts became acting Headmistress.

The Boys' School follows a similar, successful path

Under the leadership of the lively and charismatic Sidney E. Day a School Concert soon raised the £20 needed for a piano. A plot for a school garden was identified, a gardening syllabus created and garden tools purchased, including a wheelbarrow. The curriculum was immediately more lively and inviting. 1927 got away at great pace. Mr Day's interest in sport and his own involvement with School teams made the kind of difference referred to in Stanley Craske's memory of the school at that time. That view was endorsed by the HMI report of that year.

During the following years there were a number of changes in education for teachers, particularly Headteachers, to cope with. For example pupil teachers (PTs) awaiting college places were more numerous in all schools.

Class teachers and Headteachers (in all three schools the Head was both) had more paperwork to complete with reports and forms. The timetable was adjusted to incorporate 'specialisation', as in the Girls' School, with the inclusion of woodwork, metalwork and gardening. Inspectors visited to demonstrate practically how these subjects might be delivered.

In 1928 a mumps epidemic hit the school.

At this time the norm was for School Managers to be consulted on such issues as timetable alterations, holidays for 'treats', (usually Sunday School outings) and changes in opening and closing times. The Headteacher was very much their servant rather than a partner. Nevertheless at Sheringham the relationship was good. Mr Day seems to have been the spokesperson for all when necessary.

By 1929 parent access to teachers and the school was much more open than earlier. They were invited to Open Days and Sports Days plus the concerts, plays and pantomimes which were produced.

In 1930 'outside schools' were using the handcraft facilities. On November 11 the broadcast from the Cenotaph in London was heard on the School's five-valve portable radio. 1930 begins with some admissions to the School roll from Upper Sheringham bringing the number on roll to 147 at that time

Outside visits become more regular; for example *'Top Class visited Sheringham Station to see the new Eastern Belle'*. Regarding teaching techniques, Mr Day talked to staff about the teaching of arithmetic; he also attended a refresher course at Norwich. Was this the beginning of 'in-service training' for teachers?

In 1933 *'92% of the pupils took part in the School Concert at the Concert Hall'* (now the Masonic Hall on Cromer Road), and in September a Mr Gascoigne 'lectured this morning on alcohol'. In 1934 the top class visited the Telephone Exchange *'as an educational visit'*. (Previously 'outings'.) Later in the year scarlet fever reared its head again.

Mr Day attended a Science Course for Senior Schools and was invited to speak to colleagues at a Handcraft Course about the merits of that subject.

By the end of 1934 the following 'specialisms' were on offer at the Boys' School to senior pupils: Art, History, Geography, Science, Gardening, Woodwork, Bookbinding and Games. The School was organised into four houses.

Up to the start of World War 2 all three schools continued their development. The National Milk Scheme was introduced with 75% of the pupils receiving 1/3 pint of milk daily. The cost was a half-penny a day. A lower cost was requested for needy families.

Headteachers attended a variety of courses with the School Managers supporting this desire to progress.

The King's Silver Jubilee replaced the Empire Day celebrations, while the Girls' and Boys' schools combined athletics team continued to beat all comers. To underline their success two girls were good enough to compete in the National Sports at Kettering.

Electric lighting was installed in the schools. This enabled the study of electricity to take place in science lessons.

In 1936 a Special Meeting was held to propose that Elementary Education in the district (Cromer and Sheringham) should be re-organised. It was suggested that 'All scholars of 11-plus should be educated at a school midway between the two towns or in two smaller schools, one at Sheringham and one at Cromer. After consideration the Managers decided to press on the attention of the LEA the great burden this scheme would place on the ratepayers. It was suggested that the present school building should be adapted, but if this was impractical, they favoured two schools. A more definite statement would be made when costs were presented and plans for suggested building sites were examined.

A further meeting was held in March. A new school would cost £11,000 and plans to modify would only save a few hundred pounds with an unsatisfactory result. The final decision would be made when a possible site and transport demands were settled. (The new secondary school eventually arrived on Holt Road in 1957!)

In 1937 the role of School Managers was to really 'manage' the schools, with the Headteachers having a subsidiary involvement. This changed officially in this year to a more equal partnership. At Sheringham this kind of working had already been in place since the arrival of Mr S.E. Day, Miss Wakelin and Miss Hall. These excellent Headteachers had the complete confidence of both Managers and the

Local Authority. One manager was now appointed by Norfolk County Council and a non-manager as a correspondent.

In 1938 Mr E.G. Holland was appointed correspondent. The Managers' Minute Book now appears written in small but very neat, clear handwriting. The book presents a clear impression of one who has had experience in such matters. He is a meticulous, committed servant to the schools. Such was his colleagues' belief in his abilities that they empowered him to sort out all previous records, sign requisitions, salary claims, order repairs and check Log Books. He became a trusted 'arm' of the managing body. His worth was recognised when on the resignation of Revd H.G. Thompson he was appointed as County Representative Manager.

It is worthy of note that at this time all classrooms in the schools were 'galleried' (each room having a series of steps from front to rear with desks on each). In 1938 Miss Wakelin and Mr Day requested their removal. (From personal memory, this was not achieved in the London area until 1951.)

A galleried schoolroom

The Inevitability of War

Although the year is 1938 there are clear signs of preparation for War. The school was let to various bodies under 'The Provision for Air Raid Precautions (ARP)'. Those involved at that time were: police, firemen and street wardens. This implies that all were prepared for the possibility of hostilities. Lectures on ARP were also available for groups.

In September that year the Infants' School was closed in the daytime and the Girls' and Boys' schools in the evenings for the distribution of gas-masks. Trenches were dug in the school gardens, apparently without Mr Day's *'knowledge or consideration'*. This was later explained as *'a mistake'*.

Mr Day also gave lectures in First Aid during December to Air Raid Wardens in preparation for a possible war.

In January 1939 Miss F.M.Chamberlain was appointed Head-mistress of the Girls' School. All three schools were closed from 23 January to 27 January by the Medical Officer of Health on account of *'influenza colds of heavy incidence'*. School accommodation was in continual use, the following being recorded: ARP Groups 38 times, different folk dancing groups 10 times, the Girls' Friendly Society 13 times and the Workers Educational Association (WEA) 7 times. The schools were clearly the centre of many activities.

By this time Mr S.E. Day had built up considerable credibility locally and at county level, not least for his work with the St John's Ambulance Brigade.

On April 1 1939 Miss Chamberlain took up her duties as Head of the Girls' School.

The War Years 1939 to 1945

Following the declaration of war the Clerk to the local Council (Sheringham Urban District Council) sent out letters to the schools detailing arrangements for receiving evacuees. On October 9 1939 a meeting of Managers was called and all Headteachers were invited to attend. This meeting was a vital one for it set the scene for what was to follow.

The meeting set out to discuss what should be done regarding the 'emergency re-organisation'. Mr Day spoke on behalf of the three Headteachers. In attendance were the Chairman of Norfolk Education Committee and a Mr Burton. The following arrangements were agreed:

The infants should remain in the school premises.
The girls' and infants' toilets to be roofed as shelters.
The Boys' 'shed' to be converted into a shelter. This would provide for 101 infants and 50 junior boys.
Two junior classes of girls would be accommodated in Beeston Church Hall.
Other girls would be accommodated on the ground floor at Martin Cross.
Senior boys would be accommodated at the Manor School.

Arising from the above, the Managers would 'seek power' to make shelter accommodation at Beeston Hall, Martin Cross and Manor School.

A request would be made for additional staff for the girls and infants, and to install an electric stove in the room at Martin Cross where the chimney had been blocked.

They 'urged the utmost acceleration of the shelter accommodation already agreed for the infants'.

It is clear that the 'threat' was real as far as the local schools were concerned. In January 1940 it was reported that:

170 evacuees from the Bedford area had necessitated further re-organisation.

Sheringham children were returned to the school buildings with the school furniture.

The evacuee infants shared accommodation in the school building.

Evacuee boys were placed at The Retreat.

Evacuee girls were placed at Martin Cross.

Beeston Church Hall was 'surrendered' in favour of The Retreat.

To make this all seem more secure Norfolk Education Committee provided a covering of wire-netting for the interior of all windows, and timber and sand to create shelters in the existing cloakrooms in all three school buildings.

The War had made its mark in the Sheringham Schools. Changes were necessary in the arrangements for the scholarship exams. The Managers were no longer requested to appoint invigilators; the exams were conducted in several centres of which Sheringham was one.

In a lighter vein, there were problems with soldiers drilling outside the windows of the Girls' School and with 'differences' between local children and evacuees.

In spite of these happenings a conference was called at 11 am on March 11 1940 'to discuss the provision for the safety of pupils'. The following attended: Mr Cooke (for Norfolk Education Committee, NEC), the School Managers, Miss Chamberlain, Miss Philipson (for Miss Wakelin) and Mr Day. It was unanimously agreed to suggest to NEC that:

Scholars should be dispersed in units of 30 or 60 to unoccupied houses in the Town (Sheringham, beyond the Cromer Road).

Pending negotiations the schools should be closed for a period not beyond eight and a half working days.

The Headteachers and their staffs should make arrangements for the occupation of the necessary premises.

The Managers should receive formal instructions from NEC regarding these the day following the meeting.

Dispersal of the three schools was as follows:
Boys and Infants (from 21.04.41)*

Boys to Beaumont, Hooks Hill Road, Hillcot, Abbey Road and La Mouette, The Rise.

Infants to Chancellor Cottage, Holway Road and Trevanion, The Rise.

Girls to Corner House, Holt Road, The Vicarage, Vicarage Road, Normanhurst, Hooks Hill Road. The latter was sold during their period of occupancy and Classes 4 and 5 had to return to the school (06.09.43). Morrison 'table shelters' were provided at the school.

* War began in 1939, but it was not until bombs dropped in roads very close to the school that removal was seen to be necessary. The theory was that the school building looked like a factory from the air, thus attracting the attention of German bombers.

PART TWO: THE POST-WAR YEARS

Introduction

In spite of the temporary disruption caused by the War and the 'evacuation' to houses to the south of the town, all three schools resumed their fine progress educationally.

Miss Chamberlain having left the Girls' School in April 1945 to work at Wall Hall College, training the post-war teachers under the Emergency Teacher Training Scheme, Mr S.E.Day became Head-teacher of both the Girls' and Boys' Schools. Mrs E.L.Wickham became Senior Assistant at the Girls' School.

Victory in Europe was celebrated on 8/9 May with two days holiday. This was followed in November by a further holiday (one week) for Victory in the Far East (VJ) day.

Education in Norfolk moved on with the appointment of an Adviser for Physical Education (no longer Physical Training). Closer to home the Cookery Room had a new coal range installed. Cards for 'defects and malnutrition' were introduced, supply teachers were now moved around by the LEA with no reference to the Headteacher and the 'Almond Award' took on a lower profile in the school's planning.

1946 illustrates the fresh approach to teaching with more educational visits taking place. A good example is the visit to Yarmouth which took place in November of that year to study the herring industry. (The coach, hired from Central Garage, cost £7.16 shillings). The older pupils visited the Henry Sutton Curing Factory, stood on the deck of a drifter *Dewy Rose* (oil-driven) while cargo was unloaded. They visited the cabin to experience the cramped living quarters and watched the Scottish 'fisher lassies' gutting and cleaning then packing the herrings. The route to Yarmouth took them via the Paston Tithe Barn, Bromholme Priory, Potter Heigham, North Walsham and then home. The cost was 4 shillings per pupil.

So the schools continued to prosper, although by 1947 there were accommodation problems, with 44 11-15 year-olds in one class and a closure owing to lack of fuel. This was during the period of 1947 which is remembered for the severe winter weather. (As a pupil at the Paston School at the time I recall that no trains were running to North Walsham for a week owing to the depth of snow. We had a week of winter fun in Sheringham!)

Emergency teachers in training at Wymondham (housed in the old American Hospital, now Wymondham College) arrived in the schools on Teaching Practice. These visits were regular features through 1947/8 as were those of similar groups from Keswick College in Norwich.

In the country as a whole we had become a multi-racial society, one in which traditional patterns were breaking down. One example of this was the disappearance of the old stereotypes of the sexes, based on a traditional division of labour between men and women. Most girls now expected to have a job as well as bring up a family.

Our education system adapted to these changes. The primary schools adopted approaches to learning which reflect a better understanding of children's growth and development. Extra help was being given to those whose mother tongue was not English, or who had to make the transition from a developing rural society to a more sophisticated industrial one. The comprehensive school reflected the need to educate for a different kind of society, where talents and abilities in all spheres needed to be developed and respected. The education which was appropriate for our past could not meet the needs of post-war Britain.

These were the aspirations of the new era.

The Post–war Period (to 1957)

During the evacuation period Log Book entries were scarce. Following the end of the War (WW2) and the victory celebrations the school returned to normality. 'Normality' now involved a number of additional requirements from a variety of authorities. While the practice of the Schools Medical officer of closing schools for coughs and colds 'of epidemic proportions' continued, new challenges arrived: pupil record cards, students galore, one-year emergency trained students from Wymondham, two-year trained students from London and Keswick Hall, Norwich.

By 1948 annual displays for parents were the norm; County Sports and School Sports also showed a return to the earlier vigorous physical training in the three schools.

In 1949 the post war 'bulge' of births began to reach the schools. The dining hall on Barford Road was being used as a classroom and Class 1 of the senior boys was transferred to the Youth Centre. County was asked for more classrooms to be provided.

On the brighter side, school visits, to Cromer for an opera at the town hall and further afield to London, were arranged with 133 pupils involved. The leavers' class visited Bodham Model Dairy.

Generally the 1950s showed a greater involvement of the schools beyond the town's boundaries.

In 1951 Mr S.E.Day retired after 25 years of excellent service to the school. He was succeeded by Mr A.W.James who began his career in the Boys' School under Mr Day's headship.

At this point it would be churlish of me not to add a personal note, plus one from the School Managers.

Mr S.E. Day was Headmaster of the Boys' School when both my brother and I attended the school. In 1929 my brother was Senior Boy and played the Pied Piper in the School play of that name. Myself, I owe my attendance at Paston School and therefore my future to him.

The School Managers valued his work equally highly. A special minute is recorded in the Managers' Minute Book.

The Managers desire to place on record their profound regret that the time has come when Mr Day feels he must relinquish his post as Headmaster. They are sure that his severance from the Sheringham School will be keenly felt not only by them but in even greater degree by the staff and scholars. The Managers realise also that during Mr Day's service for a quarter of a century, modern education has been marked by great evolutionary advances, entailing unusual changes and a ceaseless succession of extra-educational duties with their many attendant problems and difficulties. All these, Mr Day has solved or surmounted with distinguished ability – outstanding devotion and patience – and with an entire disregard for his own self-interest. He has therefore placed the School and its Managers under a sense of great obligation and gratitude, and they heartily hope that his retirement will be enhanced by a long period of good health and happiness. Signed R.K.Cheesewright Chairman Jan 17 1951.

(In fact Mr Day returned as a Manager some time later. My brother and I visited him at De Morley Garth in the 1980s. He remembered us both, especially *The Pied Piper*.)

In 1954 Miss Foulger (now Mrs Rushworth) retired as assistant teacher at the Infants' School, having served the school for 16 years.

In 1955 Mrs L.M.S.Moores (née Philipson) retired as Head-teacher of the Infant School and Winifred M. Bedford took on the role as Acting Headteacher.

Miss Shaw (Education Officer) visited the Infants' School to discuss arrangements for an additional class in the summer term 1956 – further evidence of the post war increase in birth rate.

January 1957 found Mrs Moores returning to duty as temporary Headteacher.

The final entry in the Infants' School Log reads *'This is the last day of this school as an Infants' School. When the school re-opens after the Summer it will be amalgamated with the Junior School'.*

On 3 September the schools were reorganised. The Juniors (7-11 years) and Infants (5-7 years) became a Primary School for pupils aged 5-11. The Senior pupils moved to the new Secondary Modern School on Holt Road. This brought about some internal redecoration and structural alterations to the buildings on the Cremer Street – George Street site.

The Primary School 1957–1976

Following the earlier introduction of Mid-day Assistants a Traffic Warden was appointed for the Cromer Road/Common Lane Crossing. This shows the increased development of housing to the south of Cromer Road. School visits became more adventurous with 32 pupils touring South-east England with Mr and Mrs James and Mr Cleall. Visits to Yarmouth and Lowestoft also took place. Classes in the Junior department were streamed A and B. School holidays, other than the main ones, appear as 'occasional days' rather than 'treats'.

In 1961 the Swimming Pool and changing rooms opened using the old girls' cookery room area. This resulted from an enormous amount of hard work by Mr A.W.James supported by staff and parents. Great effort was needed not only to raise the funds, but also to obtain the acceptance of the need and agree a site with the Local Education Authority and Norfolk County Council.

In 1962 HMI visited the Primary School to assess its performance during its first five years.

The following year brought staffing difficulties in the Infants' Department and a Post of Special Responsibility was advertised to head the department. As tended to be the norm, few of the regular staff had the experience of teaching groups now known as 'the early years'. Those who were already teaching that age-group lacked the necessary experience to lead the department. In 1964 the Infants appear also to have been 'streamed' (A and B). In 1964 Mr F. Cleall retired as Deputy Headteacher and was succeeded by Mr T.A. Green. Further staff difficulties arose at the Junior School. (This is the period when management in Primary Schools was involving staff much more in decision-making.)

By the late 1960s the influence of county staff in various areas of the curriculum is becoming evident. For example in 1968 the crafts organiser, later called 'adviser', re-equipped the old handicraft room with formica worktops and tool racks in the hope that 'more staff will find the room of much value'. This illustrates the change in the expectations of the Primary School curriculum: a step outside 'specialisms' to a more generalised approach to craftwork. The alterations to the room were followed by a course for all staff.

1962 HMI report records:

> *This school was re-organised in 1957 when the new Secondary Modern School was opened. The Infants and Juniors were then amalgamated to form the present Primary school, which now has a roll of 370 pupils between the ages of 5 and 11 years. The Infants occupy a separate block, consisting of five classrooms and a small narrow hall, which is little more than a wide corridor with classrooms on one side and coatracks and washbasins on the other. Since re-organisation various improvements have been made to the main building occupied by the Juniors. Two classrooms have been amalgamated to form a hall, a central corridor constructed and a classroom, which has been erected in the playground, adapted to form a staff-room with cloakroom facilities. On this constricted site there is also one separate classroom, a craft room and an additional room in which the Essex agility equipment is kept for use by the Infants. The Domestic Science room and adjoining classroom within the main building have been adapted to house an indoor swimming pool and provide changing rooms. Cloakrooms, washing facilities and sanitary arrangements are not satisfactory by modern standards. There is no hot water supply, the rooms containing the washbasins are small and cause congestion, and the children need to cross the playground to reach the W.Cs. The mid-day meal is cooked in a canteen a short distance from the school, and it is transported to the school for the Infant children, but the Juniors have it served in the canteen. Family service has been introduced and is working*

satisfactorily. The school is well equipped with apparatus for Physical Education and the Holt Road recreation field about a mile away is used for games.

Many of the teachers have given long service to the school, eight members having been on the staff for more than ten years, and they form a loyal and hardworking team. The school, which is well supported by Managers and parents, has engaged in many activities of social and educational value. School journeys and visits to places of interest, dance festivals, concerts and the performance of puppet plays have been undertaken with enthusiasm and the staff have given willingly of their time. Local charities have benefitted from many of these activities. The most enterprising project has been the erection of a plastic swimming pool. The raising of funds and much of the construction work has been done by pupils, staff and parents and the result is a well heated pool, very suitable for teaching purposes, which can be moved if a new school were to be built. The pool is very well used throughout the year, all Junior classes having two lessons a week, the older Infants one lesson, the younger Infants one period after school when their mothers are able to help, and youth groups use it in the evenings. Very few children will leave school at the age of eleven unable to swim and the Headmaster must be congratulated on this successful enterprise.

Upon these foundations the Juniors make satisfactory progress. There are a very few hesitant readers at the top of the school but the majority are reading fluently. Written English is generally accurate, neatly written and carefully constructed. There are, however, a number of children in the top classes whose ability in written English is low. Mechanical arithmetic is taught systematically and good results are obtained in this branch of mathematics. Although some written work is done in connection with history, geography and nature study, the possibilities were discussed of more stimulating work in these subjects which would lead to a greater use of reference books, the keeping of records, and providing interesting subjects for composition. If the children are to be encouraged to read more widely, both for information and enjoyment, more books will be required and facilities provided for their effective display.

In 1969 Miss Wright from Roughton School was appointed to the Post of Special Responsibility for Infants.

In 1971 with the national publicity given to the Primary School curriculum (*Children and their Primary Schools 1967* – see Bibliography) in the 'Plowden Report', and the HMI's comments earlier, the Headteacher felt the need to hold a Junior staff conference. There he outlined the proposals for reorganising the Primary School curriculum at Sheringham. He suggested that History, Geography and Natural Sciences should be based on topics / projects / centres of interest rather than be text book based. He explained that this approach had the merit of making Maths, English, Art and Craft part of the total and interlinked. Work could take place in long or short projects and include environmental studies. Staff divided into groups to discuss and provide feedback. It was generally agreed that this approach would benefit all and further meetings were planned. Two weeks later a further conference outlined methods of project development, preparation, use of apparatus and methods of recording. Staff record books were issued and their use discussed. While the Log records a 'Junior Staff conference' one assumes that all members of staff of pupils 5-11 were involved. It is not surprising that little evidence of this work is available, since such a radical change in methodology without 'in-service training' would have a shock effect on staff. In July 1971 Miss Wright, Head of Infants, resigned. The new school year brought about changes in admission arrangements; all who attained the age of 5 by 1972 were to be admitted. A new class was needed. In the same year the Burnham Committee (Teachers' Pay Body) created in schools of Sheringham Primary's size three posts at Scale 2 and a Scale 3 post for Head of Infants' Department. It was agreed by the Managers that the latter should be advertised. In May the post was filled by Mrs Herbert.

Other changes of staff occurred with the addition of a teacher for remedial work (now called Special Needs). 1973 brought the resignation of Mrs Herbert, who left to work for Macmillan the book publisher. No immediate appointment was made until September 1974 when Mrs C. Tyce was appointed as head of the Infants' Department. Some children of 4+ were admitted on a part-time basis. Changes were arriving rapidly – perhaps too rapidly since the Headteacher was not happy with the way that those awarded 'graded posts' acted their roles. The result was a clearer definition of those roles. 'Job specifications' came later. At this point Mr A.W. James retired (Dec. 1975) after 25 years excellent service as teacher and Headteacher. Many also remember him well through his work as a Youth Leader who motivated many young people.

New Head, New Ideas

At the start of summer term Mr M.D.Slipper, a former pupil, was appointed Headteacher following 12 years in two Primary headships in Essex. The school roll was now 539.

At this point in the story education in general, at both Primary and Secondary levels, was changing significantly. This was a nation-wide change prompted by the advent of comprehensive education and the demise of many grammar schools. In some areas this change was well underway, while in Norfolk things happened at a rather slower rate.

These changes followed the 1944 Education Act (see Appendix and earlier references) and other legislation which not only suggested reorganisation, but also a broader curriculum at primary level with more pupil-centred learning strategies. At secondary level it removed the 11+ examination in many areas, including Norfolk; Secondary Modern Schools became High Schools admitting all pupils at 11+ into one unit. Pupils were now able to take the General Certificate of Education (GCE) as well as the Certificate of Secondary Education. New teaching methods and curriculum accompanied these changes. At Sheringham pupils who previously had transferred to North Walsham and Paston High Schools did not do so unless their parents decided otherwise. All primary pupils transferred to Sheringham High School on Holt Road at 11+. The accounts which follow at primary and secondary levels in Sheringham will illustrate the effects of these changes.

A Personal Account

Since it was the author's privilege to start the implementation of these at primary level when he took over the headship from Mr A.W. James, this account will tend to be more personal. This applies equally to my successor Mr N.G. Cooker who saw the building of a new school on Cooper Road successfully achieved and the creation of an excellent reputation for the school through his dedicated efforts. His contribution, together with that of Mr Pat Dye, the Headteacher of the Secondary School, creates a continuous story told by them from 1976 to 1992. This will hopefully illustrate the united purpose shared by the two Headteachers.

For my part I came to Sheringham Primary School in April 1976. I returned 'home' in fact to the town where I was born and where my family had lived (Upper Sheringham) since the mid-1800s.

I attended the Infants' School and Junior School as did my brother. My father and grandparents attended the Upper Sheringham School. Several of my great aunts taught there. I later attended Paston School and became a teacher following National Service. My career began in East Ham E6 in 1951 (by coincidence the same year Mr James followed Mr Day as Headteacher at the All Age Boys' and Girls' School).

Mr A.W.James and Mr M.D.Slipper in 1976

My first impression of the school that I left in 1941 to go to North Walsham was that little had changed. The main alterations were that the 'shelters' were no longer used for that purpose at playtimes. One was now a classroom for infants, another a classroom for juniors (in the interim it had been a staffroom) and the third was a boiler house. The toilets were showing no signs of change at all. I had just left a 'new-build' school that I had helped to design on a 6-acre site, equipped with the best that 1969 primary education could provide. There, in seven years, with tremendous parental involvement and Managers' support we had created a heated swimming pool with changing rooms, a nature reserve using the spoil from the excavation, an adventure playground and a variety of clubs for gardening, pottery, art, music, and sports. As an act of faith both my children attended that school for their primary years.

The most striking impression gained by a tour of the classrooms and facilities made me realise that the dedicated staff were achieving a great deal in spite of limited resources. However, it was a situation in which the requirements of what I now believed to be 'good primary practice' could not be achieved. There were two problems. On the one hand no professional can work enthusiastically and successfully outside their own understanding, so their understanding needed to be modified by additional training. This 'in-service training' should be accompanied by experience of alternative practices. The County at that time did not offer too many oppor-tunities for these outside Norwich. The second was a somewhat biased perception and understanding of what might be called 'more recent teaching methods'. Nevertheless, standards were good in mathematics but less so in English (reading and written work). Behaviour was excellent, although opportunities for dialogue with teachers were restricted. Many pupils seemed conditioned to be 'seen and not heard'. Opportunities to share their own ideas and thoughts appeared limited. This contrasted sharply with the London and Essex children that I had taught for 25 years. At this point I realised and accepted the challenges (a) to get the Managers and the LEA to press for immediate improvements in the buildings, as far as practicable, and (b) to try to move staff to a more open approach to teaching that involved pupils more – a dialogue not a monologue.

A series of visits from LEA advisers and HMI followed during the first months of the new headship, and a series of staff meetings took place. In this early period the 'newcomer' was able to assess the situation in order to develop a strategy for taking the school forward. Junior years 1, 2 and 3 (now years 3, 4 and 5) were given exam-inations to decide on any rearrangements of classes for the new school year. To this end the Headteacher and Head of Infants attended a conference on First Schools at the Cambridge Institute of Education.

During July, infants' sports were held on the Cromer Road Recreation Ground and junior sports on Holt Road Recreation Ground. The Swimming Gala was also held at Runton Hill School with the previous Headteacher and his wife presenting the prizes.

As the term continued, with its usual events, a number of issues emerged. There was insufficient time given to pupils at junior level with reading difficulties (Special Needs). In consultation with the

LEA adviser the Headteacher set up a reading group which he taught daily. However, of equal concern to teachers was an issue of security. Most of the teachers possessed classroom keys which were cut from master keys. This had been authorised previously, but it was now felt that key-holders should be listed and limited. Several staff meetings resulted, also involving other discussions associated with change.

During his second term the Headteacher visited the Secondary School and its prize-giving. 'O'Level courses (GCE) were now being offered as well as the CSE exams. Parents were assured that pupils at Sheringham Secondary School would have opportunities equal to those who attended Cromer Secondary School. The lack of these courses had resulted in a migration of pupils from Sheringham to that town.

At this point, with a clearer idea of what had been happening for some years in the school, the new incumbent called a staff meeting to discuss 'ways forward'. Clearly the school needed to be updated in several respects. One of these was greater parental involvement. In November 1976 an interim committee was formed, which included a local solicitor to form a draft constitution for a Parents' Association. Later that month the draft was presented and agreed at an inaugural meeting in the school.

The year ended with an excellent Festival of Christmas Carols in St Peter's Church (juniors) and an equally fine Nativity Play at St Andrew's Church (infants). Money collected was donated to the NSPCC. The usual Christmas parties completed an eventful year.

In January 1977 the Parents' Association was officially launched and in March held an Easter Fête which was an enormous success thanks to the enthusiasm of the parents and staff. This happy event was followed by the departure of two wonderful servants of the school, members of the cleaning staff. NCC policy dictated that these two cleaners, having reached the age of 65 should have their contracts terminated. Their association with the school was long and devoted.

Classes in the school, previously 'streamed' A and B were given the Year number and the teacher's name. The school moved a few steps towards a more 'egalitarian' approach, with language development and reading a high priority. To this end in May, Charles Causley (poet) visited the school to speak with 3rd and 4th Year classes. At that time poetry was seen by many as of little importance.

June brought a host of activities celebrating the Jubilee of Her Majesty the Queen Elizabeth II. Among these were a ride on the North Norfolk Railway and the production of commemorative mugs bearing the Royal crest and a sketch of the school. These were distributed to all pupils by two former pupils of the school, Mr Farrow and Mr Abbs, local builders. A Jubilee party completed the celebrations.

During a busy summer term the Fisheries Officer visited to talk about local fishing, the Parents' Association took a market stall and raised £70, a Year 4 class undertook an environmental study project, surveying the foreshore at Beeston Hill and two new shields (for boys' and girls' team efforts) were presented by the Chamber of Trade. The term ended in July with the Headteacher, 5 staff and 84 children lining the route at the Hewett School Norwich for the Jubilee visit by H.M. the Queen. There was also a cheese and wine party in the school canteen, arranged by the Parents' Association and attended by 80 parents and friends. The Open Evening (7-9pm) resulted in a steady flow of parents primarily interested in levels attained in basic subjects. This school year brought about a number of changes, not all of which were welcomed or applauded by many parents and some staff. However, the educational world was changing and different approaches to learning and relationships with pupils were required; these needed the close involvement of the teachers with pupils and parents, a closeness of which some staff were apprehensive. Nevertheless, the School was on the road to change.

For some time following my arrival, having opened a new school in Essex in 1969, I was concerned about the school premises. I questioned their adequacy for teaching pupils appropriately in the 1970s and, in some respects, their safety for all involved. These concerned the lack of reasonably sized classrooms, a playing field and the very poor electrical installations. With the support of the LEA a number of radical changes were needed. In the junior buildings the cloakrooms should be converted to a library and a staff/remedial group room, and the cloak pegs should be relocated in the wide corridors. The entire school, both buildings, infants' and juniors' needed to be re-wired, with adequate 13 amp outlets, television and radio sockets and fluorescent lighting. The earlier 3 x 150w bulbs were painfully inadequate for teaching pupils during the darker hours of autumn and winter. Not only this, but in September 1977 overloading of the electrical system had resulted in a melting fuse box area in one junior classroom. School Managers approached the LEA on these issues. These measures could only be 'stop-gap' while pressure was exerted for new premises.

Parental input continued apace, with curtains being provided for the junior hall. Success was slowly achieved in the new relationship, in spite of significant initial resistance.

In November 1977 a meeting of Headteachers was called at Northern Area Office, North Walsham, to discuss 1. The Green Paper (see Appendix) 2. The Taylor Report (see Appendix) and 3. Reorganisation of schools/staffing. The outcome of this meeting, reported by the Headteacher to the School Managers, was that the Managers should write to the Area Officer, County Officer and Chair of Education Committee on the issues raised, including the need for massive electrical work. Developments in Secondary Education were also discussed (elimination of the Grammar Schools and the introduction of Comprehensive Schools). It was felt that the costs and the resolution of these issues might be high, so they should be considered together.

In December a staff meeting was held to discuss:
1. Comprehensive education in Sheringham, Cromer and North Walsham
2. The Taylor Report's implications
3. Projected changes in Sheringham Primary School regarding streaming 1978-79 / 1979-80

Later that month the Headteacher visited the Area Office to discuss staffing, in-service training and associated matters.

The eventful 1977 ended with work on the school buildings. The girls', infants' and junior boys' toilet areas were covered in and all the electrical work, including a fire alarm system was scheduled for spring half term onward, the work being undertaken by Mann Egerton; automatic door closures were also to be fitted. The annual junior carol service, now including a nativity scene, took place in a packed church at St Peter's and the infants' nativity at St Andrew's also presented in an overcrowded church. Junior parties included films, 'The Ring of Bright Water' and 'Cartoon Parade', while the infants enjoyed a visit from Father Christmas (alias John Peacock, manager of Lloyds Bank) to distribute presents. 'Roland' also ran a disco for junior pupils. Proceeds on these church occasions went to the League of Pity.

The Inadequacies of the Buildings are further underlined

As 1978 unravelled it became clear that, in spite of all the agreed improvements and rearrangements, the inadequacies of the present site of Sheringham Primary could not be altogether overcome. A number of difficulties were highlighted. The school, previously built for a teacher-centred, formal style of teaching, would have to be designed for a more pupil-centred approach.

The year 1978 further exposed the inadequacies and age of the building when on 30 January the heating system failed and with classrooms at 40-44°F the school was closed. A leak was discovered under the boys' playground. School reopened on 1 February following playground excavations and repairs. This month also brought the re-wiring of the school with VHF/TV outlets and Fire Alarm System. This happened during the term, causing considerable disruption.

In March the Chair of the Education Committee met Managers and Headteacher to discuss reorganisation and middle school provision. (Later this was seen as inappropriate for Sheringham). This was followed in April with an additional teacher for the summer term. This enabled the head of infants, Mrs C. Tyce, to assess levels of basic subjects in her department. She was also enabled to work with juniors in the afternoons. It was hoped that some understanding of other teaching methods might result or, at least some discussion of methodology would ensue and improve continuity.

All the expected annual events took place with the addition of a play by the juniors entitled 'Alvida and the Magician's Cape'. However, numbers were increasing and a mobile classroom unit was necessary. Number on roll was now 600. This additional classroom occupied part of the boys' playground adjacent to the school entrance. Here an essential addition to the teaching area meant reduction of playground space.

I had some concerns regarding my expectation that teachers would have to change their attitudes to teaching and employ different styles. This was particularly so with those who were long-serving, loyal, hard-working members of staff. I resolved to spend much of the summer term observing teachers and discussing my observations with them. Following this, the matter of in-service training was discussed with Managers and the Area Officer. With some reservations a strategy for the school year 1978–79 was decided.

On June 12 1978 I attended a meeting of the Northern Area Advisory Sub-Committee to discuss the provision of a new Primary School for Sheringham. With this prospect in mind the Managers agreed to sell a second site in Nelson Road/Lawson Way and then 'new build' on the other available site to the rear of the High School.

This seemed to me the best option: to concentrate the town's educational facilities on one large site. The disadvantage was that pupils from Lawson Way would need to be provided with transport to school.

On 13 June 1978 the outcome of the meeting of the previous day was announced:

1. that the High School would be extended to 600 places
2. that a new Primary School should be built on the Holway Road site (now Cooper Road) and the present site sold. Estimated cost of the school (450 places) £256,397. At the same time the Lawson Way site was declared surplus to needs.

These were the projections for a 5-year building programme for the period 1980/84.

Parent involvement continued apace. A sponsored pentathlon was held at the High School site (then called Secondary School) organised by the PTA. £1300 was hoped for to fund the school library.

On June 20 a staff meeting was held to discuss my proposals for a change in arrangements for the next school year's classes. All classes in the Junior Department would be unstreamed. This provoked a strong reaction from Junior staff. Following discussion it was agreed that a parents meeting should be held to find out their views. Prior to that meeting a number of parents made personal representations and some stated that they intended to withdraw their children from the school when it was realised that my strong views on the matter would prevail. The meeting itself centred on the reasons for the changes; I was firmly supported by the Area Officer and opposed by the 'locals', but warmly supported by the 'newcomers'. In spite of all this, the PTA pentathlon had raised £1040.37 by July 7.

One area which I felt needed considerable work was the link between Primary and Secondary school. Following an introduction to the newly appointed head of that school, Mr Pat Dye, we exchanged visits. I had the opportunity to follow up the progress of the previous year's transfer group and he was able to see what the Primary School was doing. We exchanged views on future plans for our schools.

The school year ended with an Open Day. Parents were invited to specific activities at specific times. They were also able to visit classrooms at any time during the working day. This provoked an excellent response from parents able to visit the campus on an 'easy access' basis. The very eventful school year ended with me taking the final Infants' Assembly. Later came a Leavers' Disco and a PTA

Hawaiian evening, a Disco/Dance 8 pm–11 pm in the Junior Hall. Sixty parents attended this activity.

My final term was a very demanding one. I had 'set so many balls rolling' that I spent numerous hours of the holiday visiting the school to oversee the work in the Infants' Department where electrical work was continuing. There was also the aftermath of the heating repairs. The playground still required re-surfacing. It was also unclear when the mobile classroom would be arriving. (The County mills grind slowly, but perhaps I am impatient.)

During the summer holiday Mrs G. Munro resigned through ill-health. The School would miss the presence and deep concern for her pupils of this fine teacher. She served the School excellently for many years.

At the start of this crucial term, in spite of repeated requests from the Chairman of Managers (Revd Astin) and myself there was still work outstanding. However an additional teacher had been provided and enabled the Head of Infants to work with Juniors, improve continuity and administer her department more effectively. Some progress was being made.

By the end of September the re-wiring was complete. The promised mobile classroom was still not on site. I was told that 'planning permission was delayed'. Time was of the essence; I was due to take up my new post in January. There was much to chase up to make agreed changes into reality for my successor.

The re-development of the cloaks areas still left the coat-pegs to be re-positioned.

A series of meetings to agree target levels for mathematics at the point of transfer to secondary education had to be completed.

Visits by staff to examine reading materials for Infants and Lower Juniors with a view to providing a core scheme and colour-coding of books through to Junior level. This was intended to promote a free exchange of materials, information and expertise. Sharing between departments and parallel classes was rare at the time.

A similar situation in mathematics existed which was to be explored.

On a more pleasant if nostalgic note, Mrs Moores (formerly Headmistress of the Infants' School until 1957) visited the school to thank the Secondary School for their work in refurbishing the Infants' rocking horse (circa 1894). Many 'locals', including myself, had enjoyed this 'beast' over many years. The woodwork department had completed the restoration to an excellent standard; it can serve the school for many more years. The PTA (later Friends of Sheringham Primary School) met the costs.

As Christmas approached the juniors rehearsed and presented *'Torum and the Star Kings'*, a costumed version of the Time and Tune radio programme. The PTA, now well established, held a 'teach-in' that was well attended. They also sponsored a disco which was attended by over 150 pupils. This event was also a great success.

The Carol and Nativity services were held, a Christmas Party and a visit from Father Christmas for the Infants and film shows for both Departments.

After a relatively short time as Headteacher, I relinquished the post to take up the task of Senior County Adviser/Inspector for Primary Schools in January 1979. I sincerely hoped that the several changes of direction taken in the three years of my stay would enable my successor to continue and complete (if it ever can be) the job of changing the thinking and attitudes of teachers and other staff in educating the children of Sheringham for 'tomorrow'.

My final Log Book entry is as follows: *My short period as head teacher of this School has taught me much about attitudes generally and of those involved in education in particular. Hopefully this will serve me well in my county-wide role with Primary Schools.* (M.D.S. 12/78)

Another New Head – Norman Cooker

The following is an account of the period of Norman Cooker's headship from 1979 to 1992.

I first came to Sheringham Primary School on 28th January 1979 when I was among the candidates being invited for interview for the vacant post of Headteacher created by Michael Slipper's departure to the Norfolk Advisory Service. It was a bleak wintry day. Snow covered the playground although some meagre walkways had been cleared. I had arrived thirty minutes late. It was not a good introduction.

Somewhat to my surprise I was successful in my interview and some weeks later I became Headteacher of Sheringham County Primary School. I succeeded Tom Green, a revered deputy of very long standing, who had been acting head since the departure of Mike Slipper.

Thirteen years of happy involvement in the education of the young people of Sheringham resulted. It was interesting, initially, to compare the development and progress of Sheringham children with those I had taught in other schools in London and Kent. I found that Sheringham children made good progress in mathematics, but they compared less favourably in reading and writing. Generally, across the curriculum, standards were good despite a lack of resources. The behaviour of the children was excellent, although some of the enthusiasm of the London child I had experienced was less apparent. Sheringham children appeared less easy to motivate but easier to 'condition' and more prepared to go along with what the teacher said. It was all quite an interesting change.

Sheringham Primary School in Cremer Street (closed in 1986)

The school building, dating from 1906, was unbelievable, having four classrooms in converted buildings, two former cycle sheds, one former dental surgery and another more reminiscent of a sizeable greenhouse. Other classrooms were very small and only eleven could be considered of acceptable size. As there were eighteen classes, much juggling of furniture and adjusting of class numbers to suit the size of the room rather than the needs of the pupils proved continually necessary. All this on a site that was less than a quarter of the size deemed acceptable by Department of Education building regulations for a school of Sheringham's size.

However, there were undoubted consolations. The main building had a unique architectural charm despite its outside toilets. It had an indoor swimming pool, built by the efforts of parents and staff in A.W.James' time as head, housed in a former domestic science room from the time when the school had been an all-age school. It had a craft room, again from those times.

Nevertheless, it was a building and site ill-suited to the requirements of modern primary education and was viewed with some surprise by one coming from a range of schools which had been far better endowed. The traditional 'shannock' [a term for a native of Sheringham' now rarely used] and the young mums delivering their children to school and able to proceed along to the very convenient shops in the centre of the town thought it was quite adequate. After all, many had gone to the school and 'look what it did for them.' There was the promise, however, of a new school, although at that stage, in April 1979, it appeared to be a very remote prospect.

In 1980 the governing body of the school (Governors now managed the school and not Managers) took the quite courageous decision to highlight the inadequacies of the school building. School Governors normally prefer to highlight the positive qualities of their school but they had become very perturbed to discover that the promised rebuilding of the school had become less of a priority and the school was now eighth in the list of Norfolk's possible school replacement projects and in the opinion of the Governors and staff this was far too low.

Mrs Margaret English, who lived in Sheringham and was extremely aware of the needs of the town, was the county councillor on the governing body. She was in due course awarded the OBE for her work as a county councillor. She agreed to be our first line of attack and accordingly at the Norfolk Education Committee meeting on 5th November 1980 produced the fireworks necessary, having been briefed with the various inadequacies of the school building then serving the education of 480 children. The media reacted. The *Eastern Daily Press* reporter came to talk to the chairman of Governors, the Revd Ron Astin, and the Headteacher. Anglia Television filmed a variety of impressions of the school. In both instances the resulting articles were fair and examples of good, objective reporting.

The campaign continued with a meeting, addressed by Margaret English, set-up by the PTA for parents, many of whom had been appalled by the information conveyed in the media reports. There had been little awareness of how poor were the working conditions and how vital it was to improve the educational facilities for the younger children of Sheringham. The following week Michael Edwards, the Chief Education Officer for the county, visited, to view the inadequacies of the school site for himself, and made a very vigorous and thorough inspection. Next, very carefully composed letters from the Governors and from the P.T.A. were sent to all members of the county education committee. The campaign for a new school had begun and never lost its momentum thanks to the efforts of the Governors led by Revd Astin, Mrs English and Brian Wilson, who so successfully brought the efforts of the PTA to the campaign with the important help of Denise Lattaway.

In her then role of PTA Secretary Denise produced, with Brian Wilson's help, the very professionally printed booklet making the case to the Norfolk County Councillors for a new primary school for Sheringham. Although we all know how much the town was indebted to Peggy English for our getting the new school, our case was also very clearly made, through Denise's organisation, by all the Councillors receiving their personal copy of the booklet just before the decisive County Council meeting. Quite rightly, Denise was later elected as a parent Governor.

The campaign was to prove a long one. However, seven years later, in September 1986, the new school on its current site appeared in all its glory.

The years remaining in the old building proved to be a very pleasurable experience with some sadness, much laughter and many highlights and interesting happenings. The staff comprised an unusual mixture for those times: a large proportion of long-servers with a pleasing sprinkling of younger and enthusiastic teachers. Wise maturity mixed with youthful innovation proved the perfect mix.

Despite the lack of a field on the school site, a significant amount of physical education took place. Football was held on the field adjacent to the canteen, both some five minutes' walk from the school. Netball took place in the playground. Sports days were held on the recreation ground in Holt Road, now covered by housing. Swimming was taken by all the children, including the very youngest (with much support from parents), in the school pool and the standard at the top of the school was, in consequence, of the highest.

For example the school sent teams to the county galas with some success.

Music played a less active part in the curriculum, despite the noble efforts of two members of staff, and there seemed little county support available except for one violin teacher who visited weekly. This lack of music provision was true across most Norfolk schools, apart from Norwich, which had a long tradition of providing cultural opportunities for its schools. It is a source of some pride that Sheringham became an oasis for musically talented children to develop their skills. In September 1980 the Sheringham Music School began and continued for ten years providing a much-needed addition to musical opportunities for the children of Sheringham and the local area.

A class in the old school in George Street, previously the old 'Boys' School'

Craft had a firm place on the timetable, taught in a traditional but wide-ranging manner, encouraging a variety of skills. Although the craft room was relatively well equipped, the encouragement of primary craft skills within the classroom became an important aim, supported by several very gifted teachers.

The one big weakness was the lack of a usable school library for reference purposes and a general lack of books, both good quality fiction and reference material for most areas of the curriculum. Early efforts to overcome this had been made by my predecessor, but only limited funds were available. Reading for pleasure did not hold a high place in the activities of most staff or many children or their parents.

Two particular areas of the curriculum became highlighted at the old school in the early eighties. Classroom-based science with input from the UEA and a local science group initiative offered excellent teaching ideas. The first official provision of a computer came to the school on 16th March 1983. It was a BBC B computer paid for from PTA funds costing £325, and was part of the Department of Industry offer to schools.

The parent-teacher association had been set up by my predecessor and became an important part of the life of the school. The committee, composed of dedicated supporters of the school, keen to assist the children and staff in any way, was led by a succession of excellent chair-persons. The committee met regularly, gave sensible advice about parental attitudes, raised thousands of pounds for the school, organized annual programmes of activities including Christmas fairs and summer fêtes, which the children thoroughly enjoyed and participated in. Some PTAs become difficult and over-ambitious. Sheringham Primary School's PTA, during these years, was a model of what such an association should be.

I was fortunate to be able to inherit as Headteacher various traditional annual highlights, which were often an outstanding, albeit sometimes slightly casual, addition to the work of the school. At Christmas the Infant Department held Nativity productions at St Andrew's Church, aiming, and invariably succeeding, in including all the children within the department. The Junior Department held its much more formal and carefully produced carol services in St Peter's Church. The annual school journey usually to How Hill but also to other venues was a well-established tradition. Day visits to numerous venues by all the year groups were arranged annually. Regular drama productions of high quality were produced from within the junior department. There was involvement in netball, football and cricket tournaments. Cycling proficiency training, given by the Sheringham police, was an important provision for junior children to develop appropriate skills to enable them to cycle to school safely.

Various highlights illuminated the work of the school. Book weeks with visiting speakers became an annual occurrence, with activities such as fancy dress parades in the dress of various fictional characters an additional offshoot. The Infants' Department Easter bonnet parade around the town, which brought out the millinery skills of many parents, was an established occasion, much appreciated by Sheringham residents. Various cultural visits occurred including one from Kent Opera performing arias from *Don Giovanni* which filled the old school hall with a resonance and quality much appreciated by the children and staff; another came from the Puppet Theatre in Norwich. Musical performances, notably by visiting instrumental groups, were popular; even a visit from the actor who had performed Darth Vader in Star Wars who was employed by the council to give road safety advice to the children.

Probably the most important addition to the work of the school came through two extra-curricular processes. First, the school developed a remarkable range of out-of-school club activities. These developed over the years and were a strong part of the traditions of the school even in the old building where facilities were not too helpful. Once the school moved to the new building in Cooper Road the clubs became wider-ranging covering many skills and interests of both staff and pupils alike. The clubs were maintained even when stopping extra-curricular activities was used as a weapon in the campaign to improve teachers' salaries. Later many teachers used the demands of the National Curriculum as an excuse not to be involved in out-of-school activities. This showed a lack of appreciation of how children can be better motivated if you have some rapport with them, often brought about by being involved in the relaxed atmosphere of a school club.

A list of clubs arranged in 1991 shows the following astonishing range of opportunities given by the staff to the children in the school. There were 32 separate clubs arranged weekly. Culturally based clubs were held in lace-making, art, movement & drama, tapestry, natural history, country dancing, maypole dancing and Morris dancing. Musical opportunities were given to children with the recorder (5 groups of different ability), hand-bells, two choirs, the school orchestra and a separate brass group (all these in addition to violin teaching during school time). Sporting clubs included hockey, football, basketball, chess, athletics and cricket. The list is a tribute to the professional attitude, hard work and keen awareness of the interests of children in their charge of the staff of the school. The National Curriculum and SATs have impinged very much upon the time teachers are now able and prepared to give to quality time developing the whole child.

The second important addition to the non-curricular work of the school was the setting-up of a Saturday Morning Music School in 1980. A parent, Val Crowe, a most gifted and talented musician, approached the school to hold a music school on Saturday mornings using the facilities of the school. A friend on the staff, Jane Grint, together with another teacher, not a member of the school staff, Alan Childs, helped by a secondary school pupil who lived locally, Diana Cripps, came together led by Val Crowe, to give musical opportunities to any child who wished to participate. Entirely due to the enthusiasm of these noble volunteers, the project became remarkably successful. Other volunteer helpers came. More children from the wider area joined when everyone realised what an opportunity existed. A small weekly fee was charged to purchase music. Within a very short time, sixty children were participating weekly and spent three hours every Saturday learning to play instruments, playing in instrumental groups, singing in choirs, learning musical theory and generally enjoying being musically busy.

The main organisational burden fell upon the day school and almost entirely upon Jane Grint with the help of other members of staff especially Ruth Paterson. For ten years, the lifetime of the Saturday school, they willingly gave up their Saturday mornings. In consequence the general music of the school blossomed. The Saturday Music School orchestra and the opportunity it gave for so many children to play together became very special. So gradually the school orchestra became the best primary school instrumental group certainly in Norfolk and was even recognised nationally.

Concerts were given, and a wide range of instruments purchased. Instrumental lessons were arranged to match the standard and instrument suitable for the individual. A parent donated a set of hand-bells. The whole venture was something extra special in education, looked back upon with some nostalgia for a most successful project in what can be achieved in education with enterprise, enjoyment and encouragement.

During the early eighties the campaign for a new school continued, with every opportunity being taken to ensure the case for Sheringham was kept well in the foreground. One of the problems was the size of the school; a new building for the forecast 500 children on roll would cost an amount normally set aside by Norfolk County Council for their whole school building programme. There were many primary schools in Norfolk equally in need of rebuilding or refurbishment. Nevertheless its very size gave Sheringham some advantage as the case could be made that there was the 'economy of size' factor. Town growth would bring more need in the future; the present school, built for 450 children, now has 700+. Also, land had already been set aside adjacent to the High School site; the current school site, being in the centre of the town, was ripe for development and Bodham School, whose children were to be absorbed into the new school, could also be sold. In fact the new school building cost far less than was initially calculated and the site of the old school was eventually sold for much more than expected.

The school's governing body was continually reassured by Margaret (Peggy) English that the new school would definitely be built. Somehow it was difficult to be sure, until in April 1982 a meeting at County Hall with the appointed architect, Marshall Hopkins, and representatives from the Education Department including John Christie, Assistant Education Officer and Mike Slipper, Senior County General Adviser for Primary Schools, brought together various ideas of how the new school should be designed. It was extremely encouraging, not only because it confirmed that things were really moving, but also because the incumbent Headteacher was involved in early planning. This enabled various ideas to be put forward at an early stage.

This meeting was followed almost immediately by a site meeting, where the shape of the building, the size of the classrooms and teaching spaces, the siting of the administrative block, and of the toilets, and the quality of the building materials all came up for discussion. This and all the other occasions when the new school was being planned gave much reassurance that Norfolk was now not only keen to get on with it, but genuinely prepared to have the educational input very carefully considered. During this time, to obtain as much information as possible about school buildings, visits were made to Beetley School and Sculthorpe Airfield School (built to American standards for the children of American Air force personnel). Very interesting information was made available.

During the winter of 1983-4 various events affected the school. The Revd Astin, who had been chairman of the Governors for many years, retired from both the incumbency of St Peter's and the chairmanship of the school Governors. The school might well have suffered from losing his wise counsel, but Brian Wilson, recently elected as a district councillor, who became a vigorous, sympathetic and practical supporter of everything to do with the school, replaced him as chairman. The school also lost the helpful advocacy of Mike

Slipper, who was replaced as the education department's adviser for the new school by John Scott, whose educational philosophy was geared towards middle school practices. As the new school would be considerably larger than most of Norfolk's middle schools it was thought that his advice would be more valid.

Out of the blue in January 1984 news came that the school's building was to be delayed by six months as an economy measure, saving £20,000 on Norfolk's education budget. To reduce the disappointment it was realised that it would be much easier to make the move later in the year and start a new school year in the new building in September 1986.

At last, after a very busy year, on 26th November 1984, bulldozers began to clear the site for the new school. The builders, Bullen's of Cromer, began work shortly afterwards under the day-to-day site-direction of Mr 'Happy' Newlands, whose genial and efficient foremanship caused the work to be undertaken most professionally. For the school records Tony Shipp began the proposed video of the building work with the intention of having a record from the movement of the first scoop of soil by the JCB to the entry of the first child. It was realised that the move of the school, now planned for July 1986, would require much sorting of materials and making difficult decisions about what should be kept and what discarded.

While concentrating on the education of the children already in the old school, it was felt that we should take advantage of its situation in the town and create a 'resource bank' for the new school, based on the town and its personalities. Various town personalities were invited to school to talk to the children and have their talks recorded. This developed into a whole school project about Sheringham, its environment and history, undertaken by each year-group in the school and incidentally marking the 80th birthday of the old school building. This project culminated in an exhibition open on two evenings and a Saturday in March 1986, all parts of the school being used especially the two halls. Over a thousand visitors came to the exhibition, including many former members of staff and old pupils. Various people were sent invitations to a reception held on the Friday evening and it was particularly pleasing to welcome three former Headteachers, Mrs Moores, Mr James and Mr Slipper.

The quality of the work displayed was very much appreciated by all who visited. This was epitomized by the yearly school magazine, which was printed under the title *Prime Time* in a print-off of 500, and sold out very quickly. The whole exhibition established the qualities of the old school and made a benchmark for the new.

The new Sheringham Primary School, opened in 1987.

The North-east end.

The new school seemed to take a long time to build. It was most interesting to make visits to the site, where we were made most welcome, and to appreciate the quality of the work of those responsible: Bob Cooper, the contracts manager of Bullen's, Ray Harris, the clerk of works, and 'Happy' Newlands, the site foreman, with Marshall Hopkins, the architect, over-viewing with a genial but unforgiving eye for quality and detail. By March 1986 the main structure was finished, but much fitting-out work, such as floor-covering, electrics and heating, still remained. In April 1986 a guided tour of the building by Marshall Hopkins for the school staff brought positive comments and a feeling that we were nearly there.

The old school still remained, just as large and full of life. In June we all celebrated its eightieth birthday with staff and children entertaining each other in Edwardian educational style; singing games and drill were followed by the almost inevitable parade around the town in Edwardian dress. Returning to school, we all enjoyed a birthday tea with a cake provided by Lusher's bakery and cut by Mrs Smith and Mr Henry Grice who had been pupils at the school when it first opened in 1906.

The school was extremely fortunate in being treated as a completely new school for equipment, provision and resourcing. Accordingly, if we were carefully selective, we could be a super-equipped establishment. Selecting and packing began quite early in the summer term 1986, as did discarding and rejecting. Gressenhall Rural Life Museum benefited from some old desks, equipment and classroom furniture deemed inappropriate for the new building. Old sets of readers, advertised in the education newsletter, were snapped up by schools that were keen to add to their meagre provision.

At an auction by Hanbury Williams on 27 March 1987 at South-lands Hotel the old buildings were described as:

> *Sheringham Primary and Infants School....Former school buildings occupying a valuable site of approx. 0.92 acres in the heart of the Town Centre with planning permission for re-development or conversion. The Lot comprises: Junior School Handicraft building, Infant School and outbuildings. Outline planning permission has been granted for conversion or re-development .* (Copy source: Norfolk Archive Centre)

The new school Library

The New Schools 1957 to 2004

The First New School in Sheringham 1957

The present High School, previously known as the Sheringham Secondary Modern School opened on September 3, 1957 – the accommodation for 450 boys and girls aged 11 plus. Until this School was built, pupils not transferred to the Paston Grammar School or the High School at North Walsham remained at the Cremer Street/ George Street schools until they reached the school-leaving age of 14 years. The secondary school presented a new experience for the boys and girls who had attended those schools. Since the High School opened the leaving age has risen to 16 and in spite of the new facilities provided in 1957 (and a further input during its Grant Maintained period) the school facilities are still inadequate. The High School ran a sixth form as soon as it was able, which increased demands on the existing facilities. There is now a purpose-built sixth form building, which will be described later. The High School and sixth form now (2004) have approximately 800 on roll.

With the addition of a secondary school for the older pupils, education in Sheringham took a massive step forward.

The official opening of the new school took place on Friday 7 March 1958. It was indeed an historic occasion marked by the presence of Sir Edward Boyle Bt. MP, Parliamentary Secretary to the Minister of Education. The Chairman of the Norfolk Education Committee, Sam Peel OBE, JP, the County Education Officer Dr F. Lincoln Ralphs MSc, LLB, and the Education Architect, G.W.Oak Esq. FRIBA, AMTPI, were also present.

The official programme shows a photograph of the new buildings on its front. Inside are pages showing the ground floor and first floor plans. On the ground floor are rooms marked woodwork, housecraft and rural science, plus the gymnasium and ten classrooms. On the first floor are art/craft rooms and a library, a science room, three more classrooms and a spare room. However, the most informative feature in the programme, beyond the curriculum implied by the design, is the following statement:

Norfolk Education Committee has, since the war (1939-1945), given high priority to the programme of rural re-organisation. In 1950 less than 49.2% of Norfolk children aged thirteen had any secondary education. By the end of this year (1958) it is hoped that this percentage will have been reduced to 16.6%.

This school, which we are delighted to invite the Parliamentary Secretary to open, provides accommodation for 450 boys and girls. It was erected at a cost of £224 12s.7pence per pupil place, the Ministry of Education maximum figure being £250 per place. The school has been built by H.G.Lomax & Son Ltd of Sprowston, Norwich.

With the co-operation of parents, children, colleagues and Governors, and with the advice of HM Inspectors and Ministry staff we are confident that this school will render good service to the County. We offer our thanks to all who have contributed and will contribute to its success.

At the time of the opening the Chairman of Governors was the Revd R.K. Cheesewright (Rector of Beeston Regis).

Staff: Head – Mr R.K.Knights
Deputy-Head – Miss G.C.Huntley
Senior Master – Mr E.S. Howells.

There were eighteen other members of staff.

Following its official opening in 1958, under the previous leadership, the school soon established itself as a caring, dynamic institution. Aspects of the previous Boys' and Girls' Schools were continued, none more appropriate than the Almond Award for Character. This Award commemorates the first Headmaster of the Upper Sheringham School. Evidence of this continuity can be seen on the plaque in the present High School Main Hall.

During the 1960s education underwent great change. In 1965 came a circular on Comprehensive Reorganisation and by 1977 selective education was reduced by 75%. This put new demands on the curriculum and introduced new methods of teaching.

For secondary schools came the Certificate of Secondary Education (CSE). Grammar schools had the General Certificate of Education (GCE) available to them. In this situation some schools that were non-selective also offered the GCE Examinations. These changes brought about considerable controversy over: a) what had been achieved, b) standards, c) the aims of education.

None of these masked the excellent work that was going on in schools, but it did underline some of the weaknesses in education and some unmet needs. The Document, *Education in Schools, A Consultative Document*, was presented to Parliament in July 1977. It resulted in several detailed surveys, but more especially it was a turning point in education for all schools. (The precursor of this document was Prime Minister Callaghan's speech at Ruskin College on 18 October 1976, often known as the Ruskin Speech.)

There were eight main points:

a) Secondary schools should be reorganised to eliminate selection
b) Curriculum at primary and secondary levels should be examined
c) Standards: An Assessment of Performance Unit (APU) should be set up
d) Arrangements for transition between schools should be examined
e) 'Special Needs' should be looked at
f) Teacher training, especially 'in-service', to be reviewed
g) Better career guidance should be given
h) Links with the community should be strengthened.

The implementation of a number of the above has taken considerable time. Some LEAs have undertaken all; others still have much to do.

At this point refer to the Appendix and read the document: *Education in Schools. A Consultative Document.* HMSO 1977. This Document and subsequent legislation shaped the nature of all schools post 1977. To quote the final paragraph:

The translation of these aims into classroom practice will depend upon the characteristics of individual schools and the localities they serve. Some aims vary in importance at different periods of a pupil's education; others are constant throughout. All of them apply to boys and girls. Equal opportunity does not necessarily mean identical classroom provision for boys and girls but it is essential that, in translating their aims into day to day practice, schools should not by their assumptions, decisions, or choice of teaching materials, limit the educational opportunities offered to girls.

What a change in direction! Reflect upon the pre-1914-1918 War curriculum and attitudes.

Sheringham Secondary Modern School

Twenty years passed during which time the Secondary School, under the leadership first of Mr Knights and then Mr Rowlands, had an excellent reputation. It offered courses relevant and appropriate to its status at the time and in doing so enjoyed good relationships with parents and the community it served. More distant relationships were forged with towns and communities in Europe. School journeys of great variety built upon those of the previous schools.

Within the variety of opportunities offered, music stood out in terms of quality under the leadership of John Furmage during the 1960s and 1970s. Memorable concerts were held with a wide range of music, including popular songs. Guests were invited to end of term concerts; choruses from *My Fair Lady* and comedy by 'interruption' by the head boy and his deputy were remarked upon by the local press.

In 1963 the School Band came first in the Norfolk County Music Festival, and *The Snow Queen* (Hans Anderson) was performed. The latter was described by the press as 'vivid'. In 1968 the Brass again entered the County Music festival and was judged to show 'good educational standards'. In the 1970s the Band played at the Garden Fête at The Dales and included 'a fanfare composed by one of the pupils'.

Sports, especially athletics, flourished with cross-country running reported enthusiastically by the press.

Trawling through the countless photographs and cuttings (made readily available by the school librarian) was a daunting task. There are numerous photographs taken by Mr Shaw between 1959 and 1964 which underline the continuing involvement and success of the school. Perhaps the most memorable was one taken in 1962 of a presentation of a framed picture by visitors from Koblenz to the Headteacher, Mr Knights, and Chairman of Governors (Revd Astin).

Perhaps an indication that times and attitudes were changing came in June 1971 when a sex education film was shown to parents of the Primary School. Following a large gathering of parents it was decided not to proceed with general showings, but to make the film available to parents with their children on three evenings.

It is important to remember that the general curriculum of basic subjects (literacy and numeracy) in the period to 1976 included bricklaying skills, metalwork with lathes, building simple construction kits, early carpentry skills and chemistry.

In 1977 Mr Rowlands was succeeded by Mr Pat Dye. It was to be Mr Dye's task to guide the school, now designated a High School, into the Comprehensive era.

The New Primary School on Cooper Road
by Norman Cooker

On the 23 July 1986 the new school building was handed over in an informal 'handing over the keys' ceremony when, during the school day, fourteen children attended, one from each class in the school and Christopher Wright, the youngest present, received the keys from Marshall Hopkins the project architect. The school was ours, and Norfolk education authority had done us proud, spending the sum of £870,000. Whatever euphoria was created by our new home was soon tempered by realising the huge amount of work now required to move the effects of a whole school. The next day two large removal vans and four men came from County Hall and the move began. The staff, many children and parents, worked very hard over the intervening days and the school re-opened in its new building on 9 September.

It was a remarkable exercise in voluntary help offered unstintingly. The Chairman of the Education Committee made a visit before the beginning of term when she viewed everything and made favourable comments. This resulted in a formal visit a day or two later from the Chief Architect, the Chief Executive and the Leader of the Council who appeared more than satisfied that good value for money had been achieved. A day or two later, Michael Edwards, the Chief Education Officer, visited and took the opportunity to meet the staff and thank them for all the hard work they had put in during the school holiday.

With the children and staff from the old school came nineteen children from Bodham together with teacher, Carol Ransome, the decision having been taken to close Bodham School. Some care had been taken by the education authority to alleviate the upset that closing a village school can bring to its community. The children had their designated coach to transport them to and from the new school and they were absorbed with no obvious problems. The siting of the new school also brought an additional coach from the Lawson Way part of the town to add to the coach which had always brought children from West Runton.

Everyone quickly settled into the new building, although the necessary adjustments to organisation and teaching took longer. There were some difficulties. The classrooms were too dark, necessitating the use of lights for much of the time. The screens dividing the paired classrooms did not give the flexibility that was originally thought possible. The specialist science and craft rooms, required by DES regulations at that time, had to be used as classrooms and thus they became storage centres for specialist equipment rather than specialist teaching spaces. The basement storage area at the north end of the school became subject to flooding because of the poor drainage. However the central resource area, the spacious classrooms, the large all-purpose hall and the administrative and storage wing, brought advantages to teaching and learning not previously available.

For reasons required by the authority and also by what the school thought was right, this period created the public relations opportunity of showing the building off to a wide variety of people including politicians, professional colleagues, Governors, the PTA committee, all of whom had a direct interest, but also to the local community. For the latter effort two Open Evenings were held when hundreds of people took the opportunity to visit. All of these occasions placed additional burdens on the staff who, as had happened throughout, gave themselves unstintingly.

At the suggestion of the PTA, the community showed its pleasure in having a new school by giving presents to commemorate the occasion. Twenty-eight different local groups, societies and clubs presented gifts to the school ranging from £400 from the Town Council, to an aerial photograph of the old school presented by the Trustees of the Upcher Estate. The others are too numerous to mention here, but the gifts were a source of great satisfaction to the school as evidence of the goodwill that the community of Sheringham and district felt towards the school.

The first year in the new school saw various developments in the working life of the school. First, and probably most importantly, a revision of the curriculum was needed to make the most of the new building. The four heads of department put together recommendations, which the first few months of teaching in the new building had shown to be important. Next, a most inclement January caused the school to be closed for over a week, giving the caretaker, Harry Parker, an additional burden on top of all the hard work he had undertaken so cheerfully in the transfer of the school.

The official opening of the new school took place on 18th February 1987 when the Secretary of State for Education, Kenneth Baker, performed the usual ceremonies of unveiling a plaque and planting a tree; having been entertained musically, delivered a ten-minute address to a mixed audience, endured a whirlwind tour of the school and enjoyed refreshments in the staff room, he departed.

In preparation for the retirement of Tom Green, the deputy head, interviews for his successor took place on 19th May when Mr R.J.A.Perry was appointed. The interviewing panel had been aware of how difficult it would be to replace Tom Green. He had been at the school since 1949, initially as a class teacher, but mainly as a long-serving deputy appointed in September 1965; at his retirement party later in the term, he was to receive from the Chief Education Officer a well-deserved long service award. He had a truly unique record of service to the school.

The early years in the new school were full of activities and remarkable for the range of special events organised by the staff, whose enthusiasm survived even when such initiatives as the National Curriculum and the local management of the school restricted the traditional freedom of teaching. It was a great privilege to have dedicated staff who remained focussed on the children rather than the educational systems now being applied.

The old school was eventually sold for £295,000 and Bodham School for over £100,000, so half of the cost of the new school was recouped for the benefit of other Norfolk schools.

Another new Headteacher, Miss C. Kennedy

Miss C. Kennedy was appointed Headteacher to follow Norman Cooker in the summer of 1992. Norman Cooker served the school excellently during his 13 years as Headteacher. He had taken the school from its outmoded site in the centre of the town to new purpose buildings in 1986.

Having established a more forward-looking approach in the old buildings, he made the 'new' school ready for the 21st century in the premises in Cooper Road. The school had already coped with the introduction and organisation of a National Curriculum.

The new Headteacher would have to deal with the increasing pressures of IT (Information Techn) now ICT (Information, Communication Techn), the introduction of Nursery Education (Pre-School) and a growing school population.

School records show that house points were established and stricter emphasis was placed upon school uniform. The school purchased a mini-bus for educational visits. Management plans and records of achievement and reports took on a sharp focus. Number on Roll increased again and a second mobile classroom was required. The most gratifying aspect of all this was the liaison with the High School.

In the summer of 1992, the school created its own branch of Barclays Bank, run by the children. The devolvement of funds by County and the setting up of 'business units', into which schools will buy, was introduced. Music in the school has gained in reputation. At the end of August, the government issued another Review of Education covering funding, admissions, powers of intervention for unsuccessful schools, schools working together, opting out, selection and specialisation, the LEA and morality and pastoral care.

All schools were now 'structured' staff-wise with members of staff responsible for curriculum areas – each area with its Policy document for the school. Elections were held for School Governors, a post of four years' duration. This underlined the vital role of parental involvement with their children's school.

There was a radical change in the management style of Headteachers since the 1970s. The role was no longer a dictatorial one with each member of staff working in isolation, but one of shared responsibility. Policies and roles in the school were already defined with each unit having a Senior Management Team which would identify areas needing emphasis /adjustment. These usually consisted of Head, Deputy and Heads of Department/curriculum areas. The latter part of 1992 saw Headteachers expressing concern at the overload of the National Curriculum resulting in 'children's needs not being met'.

1993 brought more curriculum documents and SATs (Standard Attainment Tests). The French Club was working well, however, arranging a 4-day educational visit to France to apply their knowledge. Mr Nick Ware was now Headteacher at the adjacent High School, Mr Patrick Dye having retired.

Another regulation came: all electrical equipment to be checked and collated under EEC Regulations. The cost will be £1,000.

Cross-school moderation for SATs was introduced, as well as in-school moderation by outsiders. The school now paid for 'welfare time' (one-to-one help for pupils with special needs) from its own budget. County funding was not available.

The School Council was formed, one pupil from each class, its aim being 'to care for and unite the school'.

The monster 'League Tables' reared its head. At a meeting in Holt local Headteachers supported the motion, 'League tables do not help children's education'. Allied to this was the forthcoming creation of the OFSTED inspection system.

Sheringham CP had reached an excellent level in a variety of sports: cricket, netball, and football and swimming. The list of 'clubs' in the school seemed endless and the involvement of parents and the community almost overwhelming when compared with other schools. Excitingly, the 'multi-cultural' aspect appeared ever more present. Music continued to hit an exceptionally high note, enhanced by association with the High School in exchange concerts, inspiring higher standards. The range of instruments had increased. (These activities continued alongside the traditional ones of the 'old' school in Cremer Street, for example Harvest Festival with distribution of produce, Carol Services and Nativity plays.)

1994. The school population continued to grow with the increasing number of houses being built by Norfolk Homes. Another mobile classroom was needed. Consideration was being given to an extension to the school in 1998. (N.B. the original 'new' school was built for 420 when the number at the 'old' school was touching 600.)

In March, Chris Woodhead (Chief HMI) spoke to Headteachers in King's Lynn about a revised National Curriculum. There were to be cut-backs on some subjects by as much as 50%. A pertinent meeting since the school was to receive its first OFSTED inspection in the autumn, coupled with Appraisal of Teachers & Headteachers – yet more pressure on schools.

There were 469 pupils on roll (NOR) and 3 pupils in the school for whom English was a second language. Funding (under section 11) was not available for them until the new financial year, but there was now an Adviser for English as a Second Language who would provide help.

1995. The OFSTED Inspection was conducted professionally and received by the school as well as could be expected. The outcome was an Action Plan for Development as required by OFSTED. 'Design and Techn.' figured in this plan. In general OFSTED gave the school 'high praise'. Specific comments revolved around the following:

The planning for Stage 1 is particularly good. At Key Stage 2 further development is required. There is a general tendency for the curriculum to focus on knowledge rather than the skills to be learned and the pupils' use of these skills in subjects such as mathematics and science is limited. There has however been significant progress since the last inspection. (1994).

Perhaps the most striking record is of an INSET day (In-Service Education & Training) for teachers of the Area Schools that 'reminded us not to harken back to what children were ten years ago but to accept what children are today'. An excellent reminder that change is inevitable – yesterday is 'history'.

Concerts were now combined with the High School – a selection of brass, recorders and woodwind, hand-bells and percussion, orchestra and choirs. There were several new awards for 'personal triumph', 'drama', girls' sports, boys' sports, as well as the Matthew Henry Achievement award (from the 'old' school in the town centre). A new award for 'music' was also presented.

Miss Kennedy attended a meeting in London arranged by NAHT (National Association of Head Teachers) and OFSTED. The outcome was the message: 'A good school has a mix of pedagogy and grouping, makes good use of expertise, teaches in subjects and topics, has a clear vision/plan and assesses itself'. (This was a message I heard in Essex in the late 1960s.)

There were no mobile classrooms available (October), but 'plans for discussion' were offered for a new extension and Nursery Unit.

For some time a variety of 'clerical' visitors had been welcomed to the school: the Salvation Army, Church of England, Quakers, Methodists and Baptists.

The PTA was re-named Friends of Sheringham Primary School. Another noticeable development was that pupils were much more involved in organising their own activities.

1996. There was a significant increase in the school population caused by the completion of many houses close to the school site. The NOR was now 471.

There was noticeably closer co-operation and more social meetings between Governors and staff. In May the nursery building was started. As always, the pupils had been involved in many outside activities, for example fêtes. They have never ceased to be an outstanding credit to their school. At the academic year end the NOR was 501, growing to 534 at the start of autumn term.

The new Nursery School was opened. The school now had its own website.

October 18, 1996, saw the official opening of Sheringham Sixth Form block by Gillian Shephard MP.

1997. In January pupils had an opportunity to meet Korean children. This followed their meeting with Japanese people last school year.

For some years the LEA had given 'patch' advice for groups of schools. The Patch Inspector (now renamed) expressed his pleasure in what he saw and expected to visit his group of schools on up to three days in an academic year.

The school expected over 80 in Reception in September. Forty have applied for the Nursery.

The 'school council' requested a 'talent show'. Items ranged from dancing to highly proficient drumming and piano performances. The Headteacher described it as 'most enjoyable'.

The focus for heads was now 'Evaluating and Monitoring the School'. The Headteacher had to be the 'inspector on site'.

A new Norfolk RE syllabus was produced. Although the emphasis was on Christianity, five other religions were also to be studied.

The annual budget was less, in real terms, for all schools this year. They had to find 2.4% of the teachers' salary increase and the new formula for funding SEN (Special Educational Needs) did not work in the school's favour. Holiday pay had now to be paid to all part-time staff (EEC ruling).

HMI visited and agreed with a colleague that music in the school was good and felt that the school should build on this with notation and composing. Credit for the high quality of music in the school went to Jane Grint.

The new classrooms were being built in April. It was notable that the school staff was attending a wide variety of courses. There were also 'in-house' training opportunities.

In July an innovative Infants' sports day was held on the High School sports field. The activities involved 'Pack your Suitcase', 'Go through the Channel Tunnel', 'Climb Mount Everest', 'The World Cup' followed by running races, kangaroo race, 'crossing the Thames' and 'journey to school'. Finally a parents' 'Surprise Race'. 'Innovative' would be an understatement.

The school year ended with a school concert and drama presentation.

1997. NOR 536 pupils. The Log suggests that there were now excellent transfer arrangements from the Primary to the High School (Year 6 to 7) with teachers getting together, joint in-service training on specific subjects and on the core subjects with interchange of teachers between schools.

The visit to France, usually for 4 or 5 days, had been become an annual event. As usual the excellent behaviour of pupils, all 41, was commented upon. To emphasise the school's multi-national visits, 20 Russian children and their teachers visited the school in November.

Dr Bryan Slater, the new Director of Education, addressed Headteachers at Aylsham. Targets for the county were 81-85% for (SATs) at KS2. (Key Stage 2=11 year olds). At that time the Norfolk levels were 62% (63% nationwide). The consultation document, 'Excellent for All', was published in November. It proposed that most children should be included in mainstream schools - a laudable philosophy but questionable in practice.

In December the Juniors' production of *Baboushka* was presented with almost 300 pupils involved. The production, which involved singing, dancing and music-making, was considered 'a good culmination to creative work'.

1998. After six years at Sheringham Primary School Miss C. Kennedy prepared to leave her headship at the end of the school year; Constance Tyce, Head of Infants, was seconded to the County for one term in the first instance. Literacy hour was introduced and new admission arrangements were announced. Those with 5th birthdays falling between September and February, were to be admitted full-time in September. Those with birthdays between March and August would enter full-time in January.

The new extension opened on February 13·

The budget for the new financial year, 1998-99, was considered 'not in the best interests of the children'. This was the first time this conclusion had been reached.

For the first time parents would attend Parents' Week with their children. Targets were to be recorded with parents and children present. Parents could also opt for personal interviews.

The new extension was officially opened on Saturday 2 May. During this month, the possibility of a SEN Unit on site was discussed (later to be Woodfields School).

On 1 July a church service was held on 'Memories'. Each child was given a mug to celebrate 100 years of St Peter's Church.

Miss C. Kennedy left the school.

1998. On 2 September Mr Dave Elliott took over the headship of the school. Much of his early headship was spent meeting representatives from the LEA and local people who wished to introduce themselves to the new Head. However, Mr Elliott was soon into the many aspects of the exciting, thriving school he had inherited, with book fairs, harvest festival services, family literary camp project and many others.

The school continued its visits associated with the curriculum that had been regular practice for many years. The sports teams continued to flourish and improve. The National Curriculum Literacy hour was now a 'fact of life' and parents were invited to hear a presentation on it. Health and Safety issues were now also a 'fact of life' in schools.

Already the new Headteacher was subject to many educational demands beyond those of his own school. It was therefore not surprising that, as with others before him, he was asked to work at County level. After a relatively short period in Sheringham, he was working from County Hall.

1999. During this year the School had its second OFSTED Inspection. The main findings were as follows:

The overall quality of the teaching is good.
The pupils have positive attitudes to learning, and their personal development is good.
The pupils' behaviour in lessons and around the school is good.
There are very good relationships amongst the pupils, and between pupils and staff.
The provision for pupils moral development is good, and there is very good provision for their social development.
The provision for children under five in the Nursery is good.
The school provides a good range of extra-curricular activities that enhance pupils' learning.
The Report concludes that the school has overcome most of the previously identified weaknesses.

Through **2000** the school worked hard to adjust to any adverse comment made in the OFSTED Report. All the activities which had become a feature of the school continued, some with outstanding success. In 2001 Sheringham celebrated 100 years of becoming a Town. (In 1901 the villages of Upper Sheringham and Lower Sheringham and Beeston all became Sheringham Town, see p.19.

Among the several celebratory activities was an outstanding musical performance delivered in St Peter's Church by the Primary School.

In 2000 the present Headteacher, Mr Dominic Cragoe, was appointed to the headship of the Primary School. He arrived with a fine record of headships in another area of Norfolk.

Early in his headship two excellent long-serving teachers retired: in 2003 Jane Grint whose tremendous contribution to the school, in music especially, cannot be praised too highly and in 2004 Tony Shipp retired who had made a tremendous contribution in sport, especially swimming, and in audio/visual/lighting work for theatre. Both were teachers of the 'old' school and made exceptional contributions across all the curricular and non-curricular work of the school. Their influence on the careers of other teachers who worked in the school was inestimable.

Sheringham CPS's place in Norfolk as seen in the results of the latest Key Stage 2 SATs (Standard Attainment Tests) is shown below as published in the *Eastern Daily Press* on 2 December 2004.

Sheringham Community Primary School is ranked 8th in the LEA (according to aggregation of percentage of pupils achieving Level 4 in Tests. Level 4 is the target level).
There are presently 86 pupils in the relevant year group (year 6)
The percentages of pupils achieving Level 4 in the subjects tested are:
> *English 93%*
> *Mathematics 95%*
> *Science 100%*
The aggregate of pupils achieving Level 4 or above in all 3 subjects for the past four years is:
> *2001....... 240*
> *2002........274*
> *2003....... 264*
> *2004........288*

Clearly great progress. The figures represent Sheringham Community Primary School as a very good school.

The lack of funding to up-date Norfolk schools at primary and secondary levels was highlighted in the *Eastern Daily Press* (13.01.04). The Headteacher of the High School at Sheringham was quoted as saying: 'The school is cramped and in need of up-dating. We could easily spend £2 million on the school'.

During the period when schools could apply for 'Grant Maintained' status the school had extra buildings added, including a

Sixth Form, but the hall and gymnasium were still inadequate for the needs of the twenty-first century at secondary level. The hall doubled as a canteen twice a day and the gym had only room for one basketball court and was not a sports hall in the best sense of those words. 'Corridors are described by the Head as crowded and the old fashioned metal windows cause problems with condensation, heat-loss and glare.'

The schools which are of more modern design and were opened during this period are:

Sheringham Community Primary School
Sheringham Sixth Form
Woodfields School and Nursery
The Pre-School Facility

The Primary School has been referred to earlier since it is the second oldest of the educational facilities on the same site on the Holt/Upper Sheringham Road, the oldest being Sheringham Secondary Modern School which began its life in 1957. This School is now Sheringham High. Unlike the earlier schools in the Town they are co-educational establishments.

Woodfields School was opened officially by HRH The Princess Royal on 10 September 2003. The Nursery Unit is adjacent but inter-connected. The previous Nursery, on the Primary School site is now the home of Bright Stars, an out-of-school club adjacent to the school. The Club was founded by Hilary Rayment who saw the need for such a club. Bright Stars provides a Breakfast Club, a School Club and a Holiday Club.

Woodfields School

This School replaces a similar school which was previously situated in Holt. At two HMI Inspections in 1996 and more recently in 2000 the Holt facilities were found to be woefully inadequate. HMI suggested urgent improvements. Norfolk LEA considered re-siting to a redundant school building which was relatively local to the Holt site; this was fortunately dismissed. The only suitable alternative was seen to be the present one. Following discussions with the two schools already on the site, Woodfields was built where it now proudly stands.

Two visits to Woodfields were enjoyed April/May 2004.

At present there are 48 pupils on the roll. These are drawn from Aylsham, Bacton, Dereham, North Walsham and Wells. The School offers education as appropriate to pupils/students aged 3-19.

At present the School awaits the publication of a Green Paper which will define the future direction of schools such as Woodfields.

As for the future, it is hoped that the the schools on the Holt Road site will develop into a 'campus' with a great deal of interchange, co-operation and emphasis on the individual.

Perhaps this is best expressed by the School through its 'Mission Statement'.

We will serve the needs of children and young people with a wide range of learning capabilities through: Putting the learner at the heart of everything we do
Believing passionately that all children and young people are entitled to high quality and enriching teaching and learning experiences
Being dedicated to ensuring success for everyone through an individual and caring approach.

We celebrate success at all levels
Value and respect everyone, this makes us strong
Open up opportunities for everyone through creative teaching and learning
Reach for the highest goals through small steps
Celebrate diversity
Involve others in our work
Continually strive to improve what we do.

We are always aware that
We are laying the foundations for the future
Our priority is to build confidence and self-esteem, so that people can have some control of their lives and contribute to society
We have high expectations of everyone
Our school is a warm and welcoming community where all continue to learn and support each other
We will ensure that there is joy in all our lives. We will listen carefully to all

On the same site......Sheringham Sixth-Form Centre

The Sixth-Form Centre had its beginnings in 1995. It is on the same site as the High School, situated to the rear of that School. It now has a purpose-built complex as a discrete unit. Much of the apparatus and equipment is 'state of the art' and equal to any in the county.

From small beginnings, when there were only 35 students starting on a limited number of courses, it had increased to 150 by 2001. This is declared to be small enough to care and cater for the individual student, while being large enough to offer a wide range of courses and other opportunities and a tutorial system which can provide guidance and pastoral support.

On Wednesday afternoons there is a leisure/skills session, giving students a chance to follow a favourite sport, learn a new skill or be involved in community work. This can involve organisations such as Break, Cromer Hospital and The Hilltop Centre. There are also opportunities within the whole school to assist Year 7 with Reading and other basic subjects.

A programme of general education is provided by Sixth Form tutors and others, such as the Careers Service.

Courses and Other Opportunities

The following were available 2002-2004:

Two Year Courses, A Levels (As and A2)
Art and Design, Bi, Business Studies, Chemistry, Computing, Design and Techn, English, French, German, General Studies, Geography, History, Mathematics, Further Mathematics, Media Studies, Music, Psychology, Sports Studies/PE and Theatre Studies.

There are also Vocational Advanced Courses, One-year Courses GNVQ Intermediate, GCSE in English Language and Mathematics.

In 2002 The Sixth Form offered a course covering Key Skills, Careers, Leisure and the Arts. Part of this course is based in the community and is externally accredited. This course is suitable for students who have complex learning difficulties. Woodfields School, which is adjacent, has its own Sixth Form (2003).

Other opportunities for education to 18+

There are other educational opportunities at a variety of places within a reasonable distance of Sheringham.

The College of West Anglia, based in King's Lynn, has an outpost in The Boulevard in Sheringham. It provides day and evening courses.

The Paston College at North Walsham offers courses from A Level onwards in many curriculum areas.

In Norwich there are many and varied courses available, day and evening, at Norwich City College.

Also in Norwich is The University of East Anglia (UEA) which provides part-time day and evening courses as well as many opportunities for degree study.

Finally, it is possible to study at home through the Open University. Much of its work is done through the home computer allowing assignments and work to be sent to your screen.

Sheringham has indeed progressed since the days of the first village school in Upper Sheringham, situated in a redundant workhouse. It should be proud of the 'campus' which is now developing on the site on the Holt-Upper Sheringham Road.

Epilogue

Norfolk as a county is an area that for many years remained relatively untouched by visitors. Most main routes by-pass the county. While we who live here are proud of the fact that we 'do different' the county has often been able to side-step areas of development that the rest of the country embraced. Road links have largely been left alone, but in the case of the railways much has been dismantled. This has also been the case with earlier educational provision.

While it is true that comparisons can be odious, it is a fact that all-age schools were appearing in the Greater London Area in the early 1950s. New schools were being built, and vacated buildings were being used to create 'mixed' schools where previously there had been separate-sex schools. Comprehensive schools were being set up in Essex in the 1960s while preserving some grammar schools. It is therefore praiseworthy that in 'catching up' in places like Sheringham, excellent groups of schools have been created on single sites where they co-operate in providing first-class education for all ages, 3+ to 18.

Norfolk as a county now also provides opportunities for all teaching and other staff to keep up with the mass of changes that are introduced with frightening regularity. These range from curriculum changes to those in the law applying to educational establishments. Developments in the media have enabled much more sharing of expertise and methodology. Even in this context it is difficult to keep up with 'the pace'.

M.D.S. 2004

Postscript: Since compiling this history I have obtained two additional pieces to add to it. One is written by my successor at the Primary School, Norman Cooker; which is included. The second is by Patrick Dye, Secondary School Head Teacher 1977-1992.

Sadly, since I started to compile this later section (the post-war 1945 onwards) Patrick has died. He did much to bring the secondary school in Sheringham toward its present, excellent level.

I add Patrick's enormous contribution as a separate entity. He gave me great support as we were both seen as making 'revolutionary changes' to Sheringham's educational provision.

PART THREE: TOWARDS COMPREHENSIVE EDUCATION IN SHERINGHAM

SHERINGHAM SECONDARY/HIGH SCHOOL: 1977 – 1992

by Patrick Dye

Introduction

When I became Head in 1977 my aim was to develop the school and move it towards an organisation offering top quality education, which I believed could best be provided through the comprehensive system. I was optimistic and pleased with the response that I received from the staff and determined that we should aim for the highest standards. Academic work would be developed where firm foundations had already been laid in the form of a good balance of GCE and CSE courses. Standards would also be high in the much wider sporting and cultural aspects of the school. I hoped to have the cooperation, support and confidence of all the parents in the Sheringham area to help me to run a school of which all could be justifiably proud.

Feeder schools

In 1977 there were six feeder schools in the catchment area, namely those at Baconsthorpe, Bodham, Edgefield, Holt, Kelling and Sheringham. A sizeable number from each of these schools, selected by the 11+ examination system, transferred to the grammar schools at Fakenham and North Walsham with some going to Wymondham College. Several also moved into local public schools – particularly Gresham's School under their privileged day-boy scheme.

The same situation existed across the county and indeed the country, in areas where selection for secondary schools was determined by the 11+ examination. However, as Sheringham had been relatively late in developing GCE O-level courses in the 1970s there was a further dilution of the academic quality of the school's intake. A large number of pupils who would have been expected to transfer here went instead to other local Secondary Modern Schools where GCE courses were already well established.

There was grave concern about the implications of this situation for the school's development, particularly as reorganisation into a Comprehensive High School lay less than 3 years ahead. (The number of such pupils 'lost' in 1977 alone was in excess of 20.) As the school was not receiving its proper proportion of the more able pupils, its financial provision was also being adversely affected. Schools were funded and staffed on a per capita basis and this was a time when the school needed to grow and develop as never before.

The Heads of the feeder primary schools all invited Patrick Dye to attend parents' meetings in their schools during his first months in the post. He described how the development of the High School would be undertaken and outlined the opportunities which that re-organisation would bring for their children; above all, he listened to their concerns. Subsequently a new scheme was launched as a result of which the parents of primary school pupils, especially those whose children were in their final year, were invited to visit the school. These visits took place during a normal working week. The parents were shown round by prefects who were able to answer, from the pupils' perspective, any questions arising during these visits. Clearly these days placed demands, even heavier than normal, on the teaching staff. However, with their support, it became possible to demonstrate to parents their high professional standards. The responses and results were very pleasing.

During the next few years almost all of the pupils from the catchment area went on to Sheringham Secondary/High School, except those selected by the 11+ examination in 1978 and 1979. The school also began to experience an inflow at 11+ from areas outside its catchment area. As a consequence, the number of pupils on the school roll, which in 1977 was around 450, rose to 660 by 1986. There was then a gentle decline during the next 6 years to about 560 due to prevailing demographic trends. Nonetheless, the influx from neighbouring areas continued as it still does today. Demographic factors had, by 1992, brought about the closure of the primary schools at Baconsthorpe, Bodham and Edgefield, their pupils being transported to the three remaining primary schools.

The Involvement of the Parents

The reputation of a school within its own community and in wider circles can be determined by many factors. These include the achievements of its pupils in examinations, success on the sports field and the quality of its extracurricular activities, particularly in such fields as music and drama. However, it is also essential for the school to have the confidence of the parents if their invaluable support is to be utilised. When parent and school work together the child is well supported. One of the benefits is a keen willingness on the part of the parents to undertake whatever is required to help the school to improve. This includes attending meetings with the teachers to discuss their child's progress. Also to consider how they could help by, for example, providing suitable facilities for the child to do homework. It is also beneficial if the school can establish a relationship with the parents based on mutual trust. Then, if the school feels the need to discuss an issue with the parents, there is likely to be a positive response to an invitation to come to meet the staff concerned.

Already, in 1977, the school had established good relations with its parents through such parents' evenings together with functions such as a biannual Careers Fair. Musical and dramatic productions and a function to celebrate the examination successes of its fifth form had also served to cement these links.

Only two changes were made to this programme in the run up to comprehensive reorganisation. First, the schedules for the various year groups were separated. Secondly the internal examinations and the issuing of the reports for each year group were coordinated with the associated parents meetings. These were held at the times in the academic year that were felt to be best for each particular year-group. For example, that for the fifth form (now called Year 11) was held towards the end of the autumn term. This left time for parents and school to give appropriate help and encouragement (sometimes a euphemism for something a little stronger!) to these pupils before they took the GCE and CSE examinations in the following summer. On the other hand the meeting for the first form (Year 7) was held towards the end of their first year when school and parents could review how well the child was coping with work at the secondary/high school. Additionally, a 'settling-in' report was compiled by each first form child's tutor after their first half-term at the school. This was accompanied by a special parents' evening to consider how the child had settled in to the new school routine and particularly to identify any anxieties that might be getting in the way of successful learning.

To try to build on this foundation and to encourage parents, and others, to become more directly involved with the school, a new organisation was established in the autumn of 1978 entitled Sheringham Secondary School Association, with the Head as its first chairman. The words 'parent' and 'teacher' were deliberately omitted from the title, the first so that anyone in the local community who wished to become involved with the school was not debarred (several Governors joined) and the second so that there was no presumption that all teachers were expected to be involved in all of its activities.

It was not altogether surprising that as soon as a committee was elected and began to meet, the parent members wanted to get on with fund-raising activities to provide extra facilities for the pupils beyond the basics provided by the government's funding. The SSSA/SHSA was particularly successful in this sphere and soon, with the help of knowledgeable parents, had purchased a bus for use in school activities. Typical of the lateral thinking that characterised these discussions, the school was soon the owner, not of the usual minibus, but of an ex-RAF bus, which meant that whole classes could be taken out on educational journeys. Several members of staff were keen to use this vehicle and quickly learnt the driving techniques to satisfy a retired bus-drivers' examiner. He kindly offered his services and his approval was required by the Head before anyone was allowed drive parties of children.

Various fund-raising events brought parents, teachers and children together mainly to raise money for school equipment or facilities. From time to time other good causes were also supported including the annual sponsored walk, of which the local Break charity was always a beneficiary. There were also social events where the various elements that make up a school community were able to enjoy themselves together.

Another aspect of the work of this Association was the provision by some members of work-experience placements for some of our older pupils. Others offered to come into the school to talk to groups of pupils about fields of activity which they might encounter on leaving school. Local employers talked about the 'world of work' and service-providers explained their roles in modern society; bankers and insurers are two that come to mind.

With the school moving into comprehensive reorganisation the SHSA (Sheringham High School Association) was to be used in another role. It became a vehicle to help parents to understand the nature of some of the subjects which their children were studying (the so-called 'modern maths' for example) and to explain the reasons for certain changes to their children's curriculum. Parents were invited to the school to hear a talk and ask questions. On other occasions they came to school for an evening when they could take part in lessons taught by the subject specialists.

Among countless other ways in which the school benefited from the time and skills of members of the SHSA was the creation of additional office space. The first appeared by the front door over a weekend - much to the consternation of the county's Schools Buildings Inspector. Happily after a little explanation over a cup of tea with the Head he agreed to ignore these new brick walls. So was created a much-needed home for the reprographic machinery needed to satisfy the appetite of the teachers for additional teaching resources.

The Internal Organisation of the School

In 1977 the school was organised as a streamed school where the forms (tutor groups) into which pupils were placed on admission were decided on an overall assessment of the pupils' academic ability. These were the classes in which they were taught for most subjects, at least for their early years in the school. Previously these forms had been labelled A, B and P. The last named, called Progress, was a smaller group of pupils identified as having special needs. The 1977 intake of pupils had also been streamed, but, a decision had been taken to use the labels X, Y and P instead.

There are of course advantages and disadvantages attached to each way in which children are placed into tutor groups on admission to their new school. The Head took the view that individual differences between pupils transferring from a number of different primary schools at age 11 could have been brought about by environmental as well as genetic factors. This would be the only chance that these children would have to make a fresh start during their compulsory schooling years. He also believed that any label attached to a child on entry to the school might be seen by the child to carry a message as to how the school was likely to regard each of them. (It might be nice, but not necessarily conducive to a hardworking attitude, for a child to realise that he/she was regarded as 'bright' and probably therefore 'good'. The opposite might certainly be less than helpful.)

During the 1970s the 'pastoral care' responsibilities which schools had begun to acquire were placing heavy burdens on form teachers/tutors and also on the senior staff. More and more agencies (Social Services, the Probation Service, the Police etc.) were expecting schools to provide written reports on particular pupils who were seen to be 'at risk' in various ways. School staff had to make time available to meet officers to discuss these issues. Perhaps even more importantly, they had to be available to meet parents at their request or the school's. These developments led to the creation of more 'middle management' posts in secondary schools. There were already Heads of Department who were responsible for the organisation and support of the teachers of their subjects throughout the school. Likewise, Heads of Lower and Upper School were appointed to take responsibility for the organisation and support of the tutors. They were in turn responsible for the welfare of the children in their groups. At Sheringham the Lower School comprised Forms 1, 2 and 3 (Years 7, 8 and 9) and the Upper School Forms 4 and 5 (Years 10 and 11).

From 1978 the new intake was placed into mixed ability tutor groups. Bright pupils and those with special needs would continue to work alongside one another for most of the week. This was a situation more closely resembling their experience in their primary schools and in the world outside the confines of the school. At times too they would be required to share tasks and recognise that they had similarities as well as differences. These tutor groups however were not arranged in a random fashion. The Head of Lower School would receive and study detailed reports from the feeder schools, and discussions would follow with our colleagues in the primary schools. This was to try to ensure that each tutor group would contain a genuine mix of abilities, and that children who particularly needed to be together would be in the same group and, by the same token, those who ought to be apart would be so. A great deal of time was given to these matters in order to provide the best possible start for each and every pupil. Later, there would be an examination of how well the children had settled into their period of secondary education.

The highly successful annual primary schools' music festival, held at the secondary/high school, had been established long before 1977. These festivals gave the primary school children not only the opportunity to create a programme of music together, but also the chance to spend a day in the school to which they would soon transfer. As a further introduction, towards the end of the summer term, the children were invited to spend a day at the school, working in the various departments. The teachers involved them in classroom activities designed to whet their appetites, kindle their enthusiasm and dispel as many anxieties as possible. On this day they met their new tutors and were taken on guided tours to help them to find their way around what, to them, often seemed to be a huge building.

For the first year these mixed ability tutor groups were also the groups in which the children were taught. This necessitated carefully structured programmes of work in all subjects. The brightest children needed to be challenged by their tasks and those with special needs would receive the specialist help that they needed. This latter was achieved in some subjects by an additional teacher, or a teacher's assistant, working with these pupils while the teacher was taking the lesson. For most of their lessons in the basic subjects of English and mathematics those with special needs would be withdrawn for specialist teaching.

As the children moved up the school the teaching groups would, if possible, be arranged according to the organisation preferred by the various Heads of Department. For some subjects this would entail setting, where the pupils would be grouped according to their abilities in that particular subject. For some other subjects the teaching groups might be arranged in bands containing a broader range of abilities than with setting. In some subject areas the teachers felt that the pupils could learn more effectively in their mixed ability tutor groups. Such a mixture of groupings provided the best way of delivering the curriculum. This was sometimes a huge challenge for the Deputy Head who was responsible for making a timetable which would work within the constraints of the number of classes, numbers in classes (room size), teachers' specialisations and classrooms available.

The Curriculum

There is a school of thought which describes 'The Curriculum' as everything that a school does. For the purposes of this book the word is taken to refer to what took place during the normal school day.

Naturally there were changes that had to be made to the curriculum as the school became a comprehensive high school in 1980. Catering for all the pupils in the catchment area obviously brought extra demands, but, with GCE courses having been running for several years by that time, the transition was relatively smooth. This larger intake, about 25 pupils in each year group, brought with it an increase in funding. Gradually the school was able to appoint additional teachers, including many who came with experience of teaching in comprehensive and grammar schools elsewhere. The new intake had more children at the top of the ability range and the school's catchment area had a relatively high proportion of very able children in the feeder primary schools. It was therefore necessary for a greater proportion of the school's capitation (the funding received from the Norfolk Education Department) to be spent on books and equipment to reflect this change in the balance of the pupils' abilities. This was an exciting time for the school. As always, it was impossible to afford all the resources desired to give the teachers the support they needed and deserved. The support of the SHSA was very helpful here, although the school tried to operate on the principle that SHSA funding should not be used to provide the basic resources (text books for example) which it was the education authority's responsibility to supply.

It was not only the comprehensive reorganisation which would influence the work of the school. In the same way that 'pastoral care' had become a feature of the role of schools, so also the manner in which our society was evolving (in the street as well as inside our schools) began to bring demands of its own. There was pressure from many directions for schools to have a 'Personal and Social Education' element in its curriculum. Accepting this need, space had to be found in the already crowded timetable to provide sessions on such topics as drugs education, religions in society, personal relations, healthy living, sex education, the threat of AIDS etc. Boys and girls also had to be encouraged to think seriously about their future needs including further education and employment. Some of the topics in the PSE scheme of work would previously have been mentioned to whole class groups during the delivery of the normal curriculum e.g. sex education in science and personal hygiene in PE. Now the general feeling was that more open discussion, involving significant input from the pupils was needed, preferably in smaller groups. For those Upper School pupils having 'special needs' this scheme was augmented by the inclusion of Pre-Vocational Studies. This was to help them to prepare for the new type of further education courses designed specifically for them, or for employment. Work experience on employers' premises formed an important part of this preparation.

With regard to the addition of more subjects to the curriculum, the only significant change in 1980 was to include a second foreign language. German was introduced alongside French which the school had been teaching for some years. Teaching styles had to be reviewed to ensure that the more able pupils were challenged by their work and motivated to achieve the best results of which they were capable. However, by far the greatest changes were still to come.

In the 1980s there were so many education 'initiatives' in the air that it was almost impossible to keep up with all of them; only a few will be mentioned here. One major change to affect high schools was the amalgamation of GCE and CSE into GCSE. This included a little tinkering with the content of the various subject syllabi, but, much greater changes in the way teachers taught and children learned and also in methods of assessment. Nowhere were these more keenly felt than in what became known as Technology, previously known as Craft, Design and Technology and before that as Woodwork, Metalwork, Home Economics, Needlecraft, Technical Drawing etc. The teachers in this department had, for years, been using the 'design and realisation' approach to the teaching of these subjects enabling children to take home high standard products that they had created. Teachers were more than a little dismayed when 'problem solving' became such a dominant part of their work that they felt there was little time left for them to equip the pupils with the necessary skills to make anything of quality.

These changes had to be addressed across the whole range of subjects studied and eventually the school had to create a senior management post of 'Co-ordinator of Information Technology and Teaching and Learning Styles'.

The new National Curriculum came along too. This impinged on what was taught and interfered with the way that individual schools had been able to maximise their particular strengths. The freedom which they had enjoyed, in most cases a well-used freedom, to allocate their time to bring about the best deal for their pupils was lost.

However, arguably the most significant changes in the curriculum of the country's schools were brought about by the microchip and the increasing availability of the computer.

In the early 1980s the Norfolk Education Department bought 6 microcomputers at a time when such items were still 'in their infancy' as far as schools were concerned. Sheringham High School was offered one of these and had no hesitation in accepting the offer. When one looks at the equipment that is available in every school and in most homes these days the primitive nature of those early machines is laughable. However, several members of the teaching staff quickly realised that it was only a matter of time before there would be a huge change in the way in which teaching and learning took place in schools. It was not long before much more sophisticated machines were available. The IT revolution was about to occur. But, how to afford the hardware was the major question facing schools. Hardly surprisingly, along came another of those initiatives, a government funded scheme called TVEI (Technical and Vocational Educational Initiative). Through this scheme high schools could get their hands on serious money to help to tool up for the computer age provided that certain criteria were met. Schools were required to submit schemes which showed how they would introduce this new technology to pupils working in virtually all areas of the curriculum from mathematics to music. Another condition was that certain 'subjects' had to be delivered in a particular manner and form. Almost all of the criteria could be met fairly easily from what the school was already doing, or wished to do given the resources, except for that in science. The school had a tradition of teaching the individual sciences - biology, chemistry, physics and rural science - all to public examination level. This was a policy which seemed to suit the pupils and also the further education institutions to which many of the pupils went on to study for their A-levels. The TVEI money could only be obtained if these subjects were replaced by Integrated Science, with the more able pupils studying the so-called 'double science'. The decision was not an easy one, but, in order to gain the benefit of being included in Norfolk's first tranche of TVEI schools, the change was made.

Having made the commitment, Sheringham's bid was accepted. During the next few years by using the TVEI money, along with a proportion of the school's own capitation and some support from the SHSA, various pieces of IT equipment were purchased by individual departments. In addition, two computer suites were equipped, each of which could accommodate a whole class of pupils. The school was fortunate to have on its teaching staff the personnel who could immediately put all this hardware to good use to enable the children to acquire the new skills associated with this technological advance. These facilities enabled all pupils to become 'computer literate' while they were in the Lower School and to make use of the whole range of electronic equipment in their studies in the Upper School. As a result some IT-based subjects began to appear in the curriculum including Business Studies and Media and Communication Studies.

Perhaps the following quotations from the school's 1992-93 Handbook will give the reader a better idea of the contents of the curriculum:-

Year 7: The children arriving in the school in September will ... follow a common curriculum (including all of the National Curriculum) which will contain the following subjects: Art, English, French, Geography, German, History, Information Technology, Mathematics, Media and Communication Studies, Music, PE, Personal and Social Education, RE, Science and Technology which will include Home Economics.

Years 10 and 11: At this end of the school our curriculum is designed to provide breadth coupled with the opportunity for some specialisation and will be delivered within the requirements of the National Curriculum. Our 'common core' contains English, Mathematics, a Modern European Foreign Language, PE, a course in Personal and Social Education, a Social Studies course (Geography, History or a combined course), Science and a Technology course. Coupled with this there is a full range of courses including Double Certificate Science and two Modern Languages from which the pupils can study subjects appropriate to their needs and interests. Throughout, due attention is paid to the results of various tests and personal assessments. Our Upper School curriculum has been designed to cater for the whole ability range including paying due attention to the needs of the most able pupils.

Such expansion of the opportunities offered to the pupils was inevitably followed by the need for yet more funding and, an even greater expense, the need for more teaching space. The original building had been erected to accommodate 450 pupils when class sizes in general were somewhat larger and the curriculum rather more restricted. Prior to 1977 the craft area had been enlarged to accommodate a needlework room, a technical drawing room and space for a variety of manual activities including brickwork and elementary motor vehicle maintenance. As the school grew in size, especially after the 1980 change of status, the conditions in the building became somewhat cramped. The inadequate accommodation included the use of several mobile classrooms, a redundant CCF hut for the teaching of music and the gutted shell of the old dental clinic for the teaching of drama and some elements of media & communication studies. Eventually a small building programme was agreed, providing two additional classrooms dedicated to modern languages teaching and a much-needed fourth science laboratory. The local education authority could not, however, be persuaded to address the difficulties of having some 600+ pupils and all the staff moving simultaneously up and down the school's one ground floor corridor several times each day. No wonder that the brilliant murals, created on the walls by pupils under the guidance of the art department, were scuffed by the passing traffic!

These new facilities were a help, but the school was looking keenly for further sources of money to extend the good work which was already under way. Members of the teaching staff were also sensing that a significant number of the Year 11 pupils would be very keen to be able to stay at Sheringham High School to undertake their Sixth Form studies; the possibility of teaching A-level courses interested many of the teachers as well.

After discussions with senior staff, the Head attended a course in Coventry which had been set up to introduce interested parties to the possible benefits of the government's scheme for awarding Grant Maintained status to certain schools. Following further discussions at the school the matter was laid before the Governors, who agreed that there would, prima facie, be significant benefits if the school could join the scheme. There followed the required period of consultation with the parents, and following their declaration of support a submission was made. In 1991/2 the application was granted and so the groundwork had been done. This would lead to the school not only having control of its own budget, but have access to various direct grants which would help it to progress the enhancement of its provision for the 11-16 school and to begin to consider the establishment of a Sixth Form in Sheringham.

Extra-curricular Activities

However brief, no history of the life and work of Sheringham Secondary/High School for the period 1977 to 1992 would be complete without reference to some of the extra-curricular activities which were an important aspect of the school's contribution to the personal development of many of its pupils.

One 'hardy annual' (of which the organisation was later taken over by the SHSA) was already in place in 1977 and put the school at the centre of the community. This was the annual sponsored walk through the woods just above Sheringham. In October 1977 some 200 pupils, parents and teachers walked up to 10 miles to raise over £1,000. This sum was shared equally, on that occasion, by the local Break charity and the school's music department. In succeeding years the school continued this walk with Break usually a beneficiary.

Musical activities were mentioned in the pre-1977 notes and the school's musicians continued to develop and flourish under the direction of successive Directors of Music. Throughout this period visiting instrumental teachers continued to be employed to teach small groups and individuals. The result was that very high grades were attained by many pupils in their formal certificated examinations. With the arrival of the all-ability intakes from 1980 onwards the standard of the music continued to develop. A large wind band and an orchestra were available to play at functions, to enter local festivals and to support the production of stage musicals. Indeed the standard of these productions, which were all sell-outs, was so high that on at least one occasion the local press published a critique analysing the performances as though they were given by professionals. This merited some very lively letters in the following edition of the *North Norfolk News*! The standard of the wind band was of such a level that one year they spent some days of a half-term holiday incarcerated in the school's hall with the Director of Music recording an audio tape for sale.

Dramatic activities were also of a very high standard with a range of productions being performed, again to packed houses. Such was the confidence of that department that well before 1992 an annual pantomime was undertaken, involving pupils and staff, for which the requests for seats always exceeded the number of performances which it was felt reasonable for the pupils to perform.

School journeys to Europe continued to feature in the programme of educational visits, and cruises to the Mediterranean were added later. When the town of Sheringham twinned with Ottemdorf, a town on the German North Sea coast, exchange visits with the schools there were inaugurated and still continue.

Joint ventures by the Art and English departments resulted in a series of school magazines full of graphics and interesting articles all prepared by the pupils. The Art department also inspired many pupils to design original Christmas cards, the best designs being selected for printing and sale.

A class of pupils designed their own one-off full-colour evening newspaper called *The Beacon*. This was accomplished under the leadership of the Co-ordinator of Information Technology & Teaching and Learning Styles assisted by some other teachers. There was some guidance from the staff at the local press office too. The basic idea was to get children using information technology in a different way and to enable pupils to put their desktop publishing skills to the test.

In the later years of this period, during the penultimate week of the summer term, Year 10 pupils undertook a week of work experience on employers' premises with the Year 10 tutors visiting them at their placements. Meanwhile the pupils of Years 7, 8 and 9 were involved in an Activities Week during which the teaching staff took groups out of school for activities ranging from horse-riding and foreign journeys to photography and fishing.

Sporting fixtures with other local schools took place throughout the years, but the greatest interest of the pupils was often reserved for the school's own inter-house sports competitions. The House system had been in place since the school was opened in 1957 and was still flourishing in 1977. For the traditional winter and summer sports, culminating in the annual athletics Sports Day, there was always a great deal of partisan support from the spectators, pupils and teachers. During the ensuing years this facet of the school's activities was continually developed. The range was extended beyond the traditional sports competitions. Minority sports, quizzes, public speaking, the ever-popular Christmas competition (with challenges including decorating a Christmas tree, singing a carol, cooking mince pies and laying a table) and other fields of endeavour were all now included. There was also a House-points trophy, pupils being able to gain House-points for good work, good citizenship etc. This whole series of House activities was particularly important on the social front as the variety of competitions provided something for everyone. Brains and brawn were working together to contribute to the success of their House. The oldest and youngest pupils had the opportunity to work together and to support one another throughout the year. There is no doubt that the House system contributed positively to the purposeful ambience in the school.

And finally, 'From the Scrapbook'– a selection of the school's activities gleaned from press cuttings

December 1977: Thanks were expressed in the letters column of the local paper to two senior classes of Sheringham Secondary School who had carried out a supervised 'Super-Womble' on Sheringham Common. They cleared up the mattresses, bicycle frames, fridges and other detritus remaining from the local bonfire night. This was praised as a good example of community service.

April 1978: Sheringham Under-15 football team was North East Norfolk League champion.

May 1978: Local pensioners went to the school to watch a preview of their production of Tom Sawyer, a play with music. Over 130 pupils were involved in the show.

November 1978: Speaking at the senior prize day the Chairman of the Governors paid tribute to the work of the school staff and praised the warm and friendly atmosphere at the school.

July 1979: An Olde English Fayre, organised by the SSSA, was held at the school and included an array of sideshows and stalls. Volunteers waited for the dubious pleasure of being strapped into a pair of old stocks to be pelted with wet sponges. The most popular target proved to be the Headmaster.

October 1979: School pupils were floating on air as their do-it-yourself hovercraft soared to success in a national competition. They took the award for the best practical innovation in the finals of the BP National Schools Hovercraft competition.

November 1979: There was a relaxing and informal atmosphere at the senior prize-giving. Instead of the seating arrangements adopted in previous years former pupils and their parents mingled freely with teachers and friends of the school. Together they enjoyed a cheese and wine buffet prepared by the home economics department.

December 1979: Pupils entertained about 30 elderly people from the area at a Christmas Party. The children raised the money for the party, senior pupils made and served the tea, the school band and first year pupils provided entertainment, second and third year girls displayed rhythmic gymnastics.

February 1980: Cheques totalling more than £1,300 resulting from the annual sponsored walk were handed over to three causes. These were Break, Save the Children Fund and the SSSA. At the same time congratulations were expressed to one of the pupils who had been selected to represent Norfolk at the All-England Cross Country Championships.

July 1980: The SSSA organised a Donkey Derby on Beeston Common. This was the first time that the school had undertaken anything on that scale.

August 1980: At the annual presentation of prizes and awards the Headmaster said that it was the end of an era for Sheringham Secondary School. Next term the school would have a new name 'Sheringham High School'.

December 1980: There was a complimentary article regarding the school's large entry for the local competition to design a poster with a road safety theme.

March 1981: Two girls held their own special fund-raising farewell at the school. They wanted to contribute something to the school before they left, so they organised a variety show which was watched by 200 pupils. The money raised went towards buying a bus for the school.

October 1981: The annual sponsored walk raised £1,000 for the Kelling Hospital Appeal and to repay loans on the school's 30-seater bus.

November 1981: At the annual presentation evening the Head complained that resources had been reduced whilst demands on teachers had been increased.

October 1982: The school's mathematical modelling club displayed their work in Sheringham's Anglia Building Society window.

November 1982: Describing the school as a community, the Head said that the pupils and the teachers were two good reasons to be cheerful about the future. Referring to the children as the nation's future, he stated that their own futures were in education. He asked whether the education budget was the right place for Norfolk County Council to be making cuts of £1.2 million.

May 1983: Pupils again took part in the Cromer & North Norfolk Festival of Music and Drama.

July 1983: Scores of ex-pupils went back to the classroom as the school celebrated its 25th anniversary. The changes in teaching methods proved a real eye-opener. Whoever would have thought that the old art and craft department would now be the Craft, Design and Technology Department? Or that popmobility and rhythmic gymnastics would ever have found their way into the PE Department? A former governor summed up the vast improvements brought about during the past quarter of a century. 'There is every possibility for the boys and girls to do the things they want to do. Beside the activities for the children, evening classes here have made a lot of difference to the town. The concerts the Salvation Army has been able to put on here have always received full cooperation.' He then unveiled a flint and concrete mosaic plaque of the school crest to commemorate the occasion. The plaque had been made at the school in the Craft, Design and Technology Department.

November 1983: Three boys, who were under 16, had been selected for the Norfolk Under-18 golf team and one boy had been selected for the Midlands cricket squad. In spite of a desperate lack of resources Sheringham High School has achieved some marvellous results and what was most encouraging was that of the 97 pupils to leave the school in the summer only two remained unemployed.

June 1984: The Under-16 and Under-14 girls' hockey teams each won their sections of the North Norfolk leagues. They went on to cap their triumphs by defeating the East Norfolk champions.

November 1984: Girls learned about careers in science and engineering in a specially equipped double-decker bus. The bus was full of information technology equipment and electronic gadgetry to persuade girls that career opportunities existed in fields traditionally dominated by men. The bus was sponsored by the Equal Opportunities Commission, the Engineering Council and the British School of Technology.

April 1985: The school's chess team (all under-16) won the Norfolk Under 18 chess title by beating Thorpe School, Wymondham College and Eaton School.

July 1985: One of the Activities Week groups participated in a week of unusual sports including water-skiing, sailing, ten-pin bowling, ice skating, squash, canoeing and beach sports. Other pupils enjoyed horse-riding, cycling and even a spot of flying.

September 1985: In a joint statement the Heads of the Primary and High Schools stated that with over a thousand children in their two schools Sheringham needed a swimming pool.

December 1985: A term of fund-raising by pupils helped to turn a cloakroom into a Fifth Form Common Room. Sheringham Town Council provided £400 to provide a computer for these pupils' use.

February 1986: About 80 pupils were involved in a production of *Oliver*.

July 1986: A school team was awarded the Norfolk Outward Bound Association's Challenge Trophy at the Royal Norfolk Show.

October 1986: Barrow loads of fresh fruit and vegetables arrived at the school when youngsters held their first harvest festival service. The produce was distributed to pensioners in Sheringham, Holt and the surrounding villages.

March 1987: Fifth Form pupils were awarded top marks for their school magazine *High Tide*. This was entered into a national competition and won £100 cash and several books for the library.

June 1987: The Alliance candidate romped home with a convincing victory in the school's mock general election.

January 1988: Some pupils went to a special media studies day at Holt Hall. They enjoyed filming their own chat show and also had a go at taking and developing photographs.

March 1988: The staff took on a group of pupils in a charity football marathon to raise funds for the Great Ormond Street Hospital where one of the boys had undergone two life-saving operations in his infancy.

October 1988: Fifth Form pupils took part in a 'Healthy Living Conference' funded by the Norwich Health Authority. The objective of this exercise in preventative medicine was for pupils to learn about diet, techniques to deal with stress, exercise for the elderly and other life skills.

October 1988: Weather maps beamed direct from space were part of the new benefit to pupils as the school was included in Norfolk's first phase of TVEI funding. As a result the school was to receive an extra £68,000 over the next four years to help to buy computers and the latest technological equipment.

November 1988: Sheringham children took the plunge at Splash for the first time.

January 1989: Barclays Bank gave £1,000 towards the cost of purchasing a new video system called the 'Domesday Project'. This marked the 900th anniversary of the original Domesday Book record. Data can be called up by pupils to enable them to study the geography or history of any area of the country.

April 1989: Thirty-two pupils with their accompanying teachers paid a return visit to Otterndorf. They experienced a marvellous week of excellent hospitality. They toured the local area, participated in lessons at the Realschule and went on trips to Hamburg and the Harz mountains.

June 1989: 140 Fourth Form pupils attended a special briefing on money matters. Eight invited speakers visited the school to run a series of workshops on financial topics.

July 1989: Forty-five members of the school band played a wide selection of pieces during concerts on a tour of North Norfolk primary schools.

September 1989: A cross-cultural exchange trip, boosted by a £500 cash grant from British Gas, took 30 pupils to the Sheffield area for the opportunity to learn about life and work in a different part of the country.

January 1990: New technology was at the forefront of a scheme which it was hoped would lure extra tourists to North Norfolk. As part of their GCSE studies some pupils were engaged in compiling data and a video film relevant to the area's holiday trade and transferring it to a computer. Three teachers at the school designed an interactive computerised system called SHIELD (Sheringham Initiative Exploring Local Data) for providing visitors with this tourist information at the touch of a button. This work was supported by a grant of £1,000 from Sheringham. The finished product was prominently situated on the platform at Norwich Railway Station. This was such innovative work for a school that it attracted the attention of the national educational press and praise from the local Euro MP.

October 1990: Pupils were filmed by the BBC as they used Ecodisc to find out about the environment, ecology and wildlife in the modern equivalent to traditional nature study. A programme researcher said, 'Sheringham is one of the few schools which is being very innovative and forward thinking with the use of Ecodisc'.

December 1990: At the annual Awards Evening the 1989 GCSE examination results were reported as being significantly better than the national statistics. The Head pointed out that these results had been achieved despite great pressures. Not only were the teachers coping with the perennial lack of resources, but they were having to introduce the National Curriculum while the switch from the old CSE and GCE tests was still settling down.

February 1991: Pupils at North Norfolk schools were suffering from the worst 'flu epidemic teachers could remember.

May 1991: Playbox, a playgroup at the school, was launched with the dual purpose of helping busy mums with young children and also giving first-hand experience to pupils studying GCSE courses involving child development.

October 1991: A piece of work by music pupils was included in a composition by a Norwich composer and performed to packed audiences at the Norfolk & Norwich Festival.

December 1991: Speaking at an awards evening the Head criticised the government's push for schools to get back to basics. The government wanted schools to test what information children could remember rather than to see how they could locate, evaluate and use information. He regarded this as a retrograde step.

March 1992: Hundreds of parents in the Sheringham area had voted in favour of their school opting out of county council control. 72% of those voting were in favour of applying for Grant Maintained status.

March 1992: The school began a feasibility study to investigate the possibility of offering post-16 education in Sheringham. If the study proved positive, the school could develop a further education centre for sixth form pupils.

June 1992: Fourth Year pupils spent the day 'marketing sweets and selling them to France' in a scene-setting session to prepare them for the outside world. The day was designed to make them more aware of the demands of commerce.

June 1992: The rhythmic beat of Third World music echoed around the school as pupils got a feel for other countries' cultures. A number of artists who were heading for the One World Festival in Norwich led the sessions. The day was partly for fun, but helped with learning right across the curriculum from music to English.

N.B. Unfortunately the written account of the work of the school in these years does not appear to have been retained in the school files or in the County Education Offices. This contained a detailed record of the school's history, development, changes and plans for the future which I wrote in reporting regularly to the Governors as Headmaster. The foregoing is, therefore, an attempt, based on my recollections, to outline some of the characteristics of Sheringham Secondary/High School in the period from 1977 to 1992.

Without these records I can recall many events and many individuals, some excellent teachers and indeed some outstanding ones. However, I have decided that it would be unfair to mention any pupils, staff and Governors by name and so run the risk of appearing to ignore the contributions of others.

Of enormous help to me throughout my time at Sheringham was the backing that I received from the Governors and the enormous support given by successive occupants of the role of Chairman. Time moves on and in a couple of years I shall have been retired from Sheringham High School for as long as I served there.

Looking back on those years I feel great pleasure and no little pride. I count myself fortunate to have spent 15 years working with a dedicated team of teachers and support staff who helped to make the school what it is today. What gives my personal reminiscences the warmest glow of all is the recollection of the caring nature and enthusiastic contributions of the children who passed through the school in those years.

January 2005

Appendix One: Headteachers

Upper Sheringham 'All age' School (1853-1949)

Mr L. W. Almond
Mr E. G. Savage
Mrs Garwood
Miss Williamson

Lower Sheringham Infants Schoolmistresses (1888-1906)

Miss Alice Parnell
Miss Emily Kent
Miss A. Worraker

The 'New' Schools on Cromer St and George St Infants, 'All Age' Boys and 'All Age' Girls (1906-1957)

Boys

Mr Hammond Smith
Mr S. E. Day (Mr Day took over the combined 'All Age' schools when Miss F.M.Chamberlain left for Wall Hall College in 1945)
Mr A. W. James (Mr James also led the two schools)

The Primary School on Cremer Street (1957-1986)

Mr A.W. James
Mr M.D. Slipper
Mr N.G. Cooker

Girls

Miss E. A. Miller
Miss M. Park
Miss J. K. Call
Miss E. M. Wheatly
Miss Hall
Miss F.M. Chamberlain (As above, Mr Day took charge of both schools in 1945 with Miss H.Watts as 'Head of Girls Department'.)

Infants

Miss A. Worraker
Mrs A. E. Tansley
Miss C. Wakelin
Miss Philipson later to become Mrs Moores

The 'New' Primary School on Cooper Road (1986+)

Mr N. G. Cooker
Miss Christine M. Kennedy
Mr Dave Elliott
Mr Dominic Cragoe

Nursery Unit (Teacher in Charge)

Hilary Rayment

Special School (2003+) (Headteacher)

Mrs Diane Witham

The New High School on Holt Road (1957)

Mr R. W. Knight
Mr O. Rowlands
Mr P. Dye (The Secondary Modern School is now a High School)
Mr N. Ware
Mr M. Goodwin
Mr Tim Roderick (09/04)

Appendix Two: Education Acts & Health Acts

1848 1st Public Health Act (Edwin Chadwick): Some type of sanitary arrangements required for every household.

1875 2nd Public Health Act (Disraeli Government): Every Council to appoint a Medical Officer of Health (MOH)

During the latter part of the 19th Century country dwellers just dug a hole and covered it with earth when full.

Earth closets – deep pits and a construction with a wooden seat. Later raised seats, at first a plain plank. These were emptied once a year with a long-handled ladle (like a large soup spoon). The waste was taken to a specially dug hole in an open field.

1897 Shanks and Company made the Victorian closet. (There is an unusual collection at King's Lynn Museum where the above mentioned can be seen.)

See also *East Anglian Privies*, Jean Turner (ISBN 1-85306-304-4)

The above Health Acts are very relevant to the schools at Upper and Lower Sheringham prior to 1906.

1870 – The Forster Education Act
Board schools to be built where there were insufficient voluntary schools. Perhaps the most significant act, which made education compulsory.
W.E.Forster established a system of elementary schools in England and Wales. Locally elected School Boards were to provide schools where there was a deficiency of schools run by the denominational bodies. This Act was the beginning of the so-called 'dual system' which still exists.

1880 an Act imposed universal compulsory schooling under the age of 10.

The 1902 Act. A.J. Balfour set up a co-ordinated national system of education administered by a central Board of Education. School Boards were abolished and replaced by Local Education Authorities (LEAs). Grammar Schools were established and free places provided for pupils from elementary schools.

The Change

The Future of Education to 16 (and later 18)

The 1944 Education Act. This required every Local Education Authority to prepare a development plan of educational needs. Norfolk's plan was complete in 1947 and contained far-reaching proposals for primary school closure and new building. In Norfolk, of 464 primary schools, 200 had been built before 1870 and 405 before 1900. New regulations were set with minimum standards for accommodation, which were: 'probably above that of any existing school and far beyond that of the vast majority of Norfolk schools at this time.'

A survey undertaken in 1946 showed that it would be impractical to bring existing schools up to the new standards. An eighteen-year programme was drawn up, but this proved to be far too ambitious. Nevertheless, the basic plan has been retained in programmes of the County Council. Some 170 primary schools have been closed since 1947.

Education was organised into three stages: Primary, Secondary and Further, and divided into grammar, technical and modern. The Board of Education was replaced by a Ministry of Education and provision was made for raising the school-leaving age from 14 to 15; it was raised to 16 in 1972. The Act remained in force for the next four decades, but selection for the different schools caused many difficulties. Labour governments from 1964 encouraged comprehensive schooling.

Children and Their Primary Schools (1967)
A report of the Central Advisory Council of Education – England (The Plowden Report)

Education in Schools A Consultative Document (1977) HMSO ISBN 010168690 0

There followed a series of 'Surveys' (Reports)

Education 5 to 9 (Department of Education and Science)
First Schools Survey (1982)

Education 9 to 12 (Department of Education and Science)
Middle Schools Survey

The National Curriculum (1987) and later revised

The Introduction of routine inspections nationally by The Office for Standards in Education (OFSTED)

The Literacy Hour (introduced 1998)

The Numeracy Hour (introduced 2000)

BIBLIOGRAPHY

Eric Austen *All That I Was...A Village Childhood in the Thirties.* ISBN 1-874739-07-2

Terry Derby *The Vile Victorians* ISBN 0-590554-66-2 – for a light-harted approach

R. Douglas-Brown *East Anglia 1942* ISBN 0-861380-56-8

A. Campbell-Errol (1970) *A History of Sheringham and Beeston Regis.* Published by the author

Alan Childs (1992) *Sheringham and Beeston*

Peter Cox (2000) *The Divided Village* ISBN 0-952481-05-7

Peter Cox (2001) *The Village Becomes a Town*

R. Douglas-Brown *East Anglia 1942* ISBN 0-861380-56-8

A. Mason *Forging the Modern Age 1900-1914* Toucan Books Ltd ISBN 0-276423-63-1

Reader's Digest Assn. Ltd *Life on The Home Front* ISBN 0-276421-20-5

Andy Reid *The Union Workhouse* (a study guide for local historians and teachers) Phillimore for British Association for Local History ISBN 0-85033-914-6. (Sections on 'schools' and 'children' are particularly interesting and relevant to this book)

M. D. Slipper *A Family History.* Unpublished

Jean Turner *No Time Like the Past* ISBN 1-85306-467-X

Peter Wade-Martins (ed.) 1994 *An Historical Atlas of Norfolk* ISBN 0-903101-60-2

Susanna Wade-Martins (1997) *A History of Norfolk* by Susanna Wade-Martins (1997) ISBN 1-860770-14-2

Susan Yaxley (ed.1986) *Sherringhamia – The Journal of Abbot Upcher 1813-16)* The Larks Press ISBN 0 948400-04-8

For more information on food rationing see the work of Marguerite Patten who worked as a food adviser in the Ministry of Food 1942-1947

See also: *Education in Schools - A Consultative Document 1977* H.M.S.O. ISBN 0-101686-90-0

INDEX